GOVERNMENT
PARTY
AND PEOPLE
IN NAZI GERMANY

Edited by Jeremy Noakes

EXETER STUDIES IN HISTORY No 2

Published by the University

Printed in Great Britain by A. Wheaton & Co. Ltd., Exeter

ISBN 0 85989 112 7

ISSN 0260-8626

Contents

Acknowledgements

The editors wish to thank Judith Saywell and Mary Laws for typing and processing the manuscripts and Seán Goddard for designing the headings. The cover was designed and drawn by Mike Rouillard.

Introduction: Government, Party and People in Nazi Germany

JEREMY NOAKES

The last years of the Weimar Republic saw German society in a process of disintegration under the centrifugal pressures unleashed by economic crisis. Social dissolution was quickly reflected in the collapse of a democratic political order whose foundations proved too weak to take the strain. The problems were deep-rooted. Essentially, they derived from the failure of the German people to develop a consensus about the fundamentals of their political order. During the years 1871-1914, the new German Reich had suffered the disruptive social effects of a phase of extremely rapid industrialization superimposed on the already disruptive political effects of national unification. The political fragmentation which resulted from this dual process of dislocation and, in particular, the failure to integrate the new industrial working class into the nation on an equitable basis, was papered over by virulent nationalism and loyalty to the monarchy. However, the lack of parliamentary government enabled the political parties to escape the responsibility of establishing a political compromise between the conflicting ideologies and interests. The political vacuum was filled, in theory, by a government and civil service which claimed to define the true interests of the nation, in practice, however, by ministers responding mainly to the pressure groups representing powerful elites - the army, the Junker landowners of East Elbia, and heavy industry - and by an irresponsible emperor.

Because of the failure of Imperial Germany to develop broadly-based parties aggregating a wide range of interests, the Weimar Republic had been confronted from the start by a large number of parties representing the divisions of interest and ideology which had characterized pre-war Germany. Moreover, after 1918, these divisions had been sharpened by the effects of war and revolution. This tendency towards political fragmentation had been exacerbated by the new electoral system which was based on an extreme form of proportional representation. During the 1920s, increasing disillusionment with the representation of their interests by the various parties had even encouraged particular pressure groups to emancipate themselves entirely from the parties with which they had previously been associated and to establish special interest parties of their own.

The Nazis based their main appeal on a promise to integrate German society in a new 'national community' (Volksgemeinschaft) and then to use the renewed strength flowing from national unity to restore Germany's position in the world. The only occasion hitherto when Germany had achieved such a sense of unity was on the outbreak of war in August 1914. Since then 'August 1914' had become a potent myth for the

German Right, an occasion when national unity had apparently been achieved without having to go through the painful economic and social reforms necessary to arrive at a more just and, therefore, more widely accepted social order. Nazism has, in fact, been aptly described as 'an attempt to reproduce the experiences of 1914 as a permanent condition'.[1]

In Hitler's view, the unity of 1914 had failed to survive because agitators working wittingly or unwittingly in the service of the Jews had undermined it by exploiting the inadequacies of the pre-war and war-time governments who had failed to deal with a fatal sickness in the German body politic. For, according to Hitler, Germany was weakened by the fact that the divisions between the German states during the nineteenth century, which had been overcome by Bismarck's creation of a united Germany, had been replaced by divisions between social classes. These divisions had been fostered and exploited by the Jews through the doctrines of Liberalism with its emphasis on the priority of the individual over the community, of democracy with its subordination of the 'creative' and 'heroic' individual to the mass, and of Marxism with its advocacy of class war. Moreover, all these doctrines preached the supreme importance of man's common humanity overriding national and racial distinctions. They stressed international ties which inevitably led to a horror of war and, therefore, to pacifism. Furthermore, by denying the significance of race, they paved the way for the Jews to establish hegemony. Owing to the weakness of pre-war governments, these 'unnatural' ideas had exercised a pervasive influence over the previous decades and had deeply entrenched themselves in German society and culture, sapping the national will. To restore German unity and morale, therefore, would now require 'internal reforms'. Hitler, however, like his Pan-German mentors, saw the 'internal reforms' which were necessary not in terms of a radical reconstruction of the economic and social order, but rather in terms of the creation of a new mentality. At the core of this new mentality would be: first, an acceptance of the 'laws of nature' of which the racial struggle and the Jewish question were of paramount importance; and secondly, a new sense of community. The divisions which had bedevilled Germany in the past and caused her recent defeat: divisions based on class, regional loyalties, and religious denomination would be overcome in an overriding and total personal commitment on the part of all Germans to a new 'national community', which would be created by the Nazi party and whose interests would be expressed through his leadership.

The very vagueness of their goals of national integration and national revival enabled the Nazis to make a broad appeal, encouraging individuals and groups to identify their own particular hopes and aspirations with the party and its leader. In other words, Nazism came to mean many things to many people. Some, particularly among party activists, saw it as a revolutionary and egalitarian movement breaking down social barriers, removing the authority of traditional elites based on birth and wealth and introducing a new and more meritocratic social order. Others, however, saw it as a movement reasserting traditional German values - above all national pride - after a period when 'un-German' ideas and political practices had been allowed to predominate. This was true of many middle class Nazi voters and many among the traditional elites.

The heterogeneity of the Nazi movement proved a distinct electoral advantage. With the appointment of Hitler as Chancellor, however, it posed massive new problems for the leadership. Hitherto, the party had been essentially a vote-winning machine. It had not needed to produce elaborate plans for government. Indeed, by committing the party to specific courses of action, involving advantages and disadvantages for particular groups, such plans would have risked alienating sections of support. After January 1933, however, choices had to be made and priorities set. Some people were bound to be disappointed. Hitler was obliged to steer a careful course between his need to retain the support of his movement, without which he would become a prisoner of the elites, and his need to retain the support of the elites, without whom he could not govern, let alone embark on a rapid programme of rearmament. Above all, he could not bring about the economic recovery which was vital if he were to increase public support and without such support he would be unlikely to remain in power for long and certainly would be unable to achieve his major goal of making Germany a world power.

The essays in this collection seek first to consider the question of how the Nazi movement set about achieving its professed aim of re-establishing political authority and reintegrating German society in a new 'national community', and second, to examine the response of the German people to those attempts. The main mechanisms for achieving political and social change were the Nazi movement on the one hand and the state apparatus on the other, and one of the main flaws at the heart of the new regime proved to be the impossibility of working out an effective relationship between the two. Having secured power, the Nazi party fell victim to its own success and to its own nature. As a movement geared primarily to the mobilization of support from members and voters, it had developed into a conglomeration of separate organizations and departments fulfilling particular functions or representing particular social and economic interests and run by a group of political entrepreneurs. These various organizations were tied loosely to a cadre political organization whose main basis was regional and which lacked a strong central apparatus.

At the core of the party's organization was the so-called Führerprinzip - the absolute authority of all leaders over their subordinates but, above all, the absolute and direct authority of the Führer himself over all other members of the party. Hitler's style of leadership had developed in a dynamic relationship with those who followed him. The peculiar relationship between leader and followers originated in the early years of the Nazi party in Munich, was then accepted by the party throughout Germany after 1925, and finally was transferred to the German nation as a whole. The particular 'charismatic' quality of Hitler's leadership was partly the result of his remarkable gifts of oratory and personality and partly a product of the Nazi propaganda machine, but it also reflected the emotional needs of his followers - those within the Nazi movement itself and those among the German people at large - in particular their hunger for leadership. After the collapse of the monarchy, the Weimar Republic had failed to win widespread acceptance let alone emotional loyalty; there emerged a vacuum of authority which could only be deeply disturbing to a nation accustomed to authoritarian modes of behaviour in its social and political life. Many people were yearning for a restoration of national pride as a key to the revival of their own self-esteem and, at the same time, were searching for strong leadership. The economic crisis of 1929-1933 created conditions in which this kind of total personal commitment to a leader figure acquired a much broader appeal. However this was not a one-way channel of emotional energy between leader and followers, for, at the same time, a growing awareness of the power of his oratory and of his political success continually reinforced Hitler's own self-confidence in his abilities and increasingly persuaded him that he was a figure marked out by destiny to achieve the national revival of Germany. This sense of destiny he then communicated to his followers, thereby reinforcing their commitment to him.

The Führerprinzip dictated both the party's style and its dynamics. Without an established hierarchy of offices with clear-cut lines of responsiblity, only the approval or disapproval of the leader could determine the relative positions and competencies of the various individuals and their organizations. Hitler, however, was extremely loath to commit himself, beyond temporary commissions, to particular individuals rather than to offices. Nor did he feel bound by such commitments. Although he made the rules, he also felt free to break them - for example to deal with a Gauleiter directly, bypassing the party headquarters. The uncertainty resulting from this situation produced endemic conflict within the party. Individuals were forced to compete with one another for the leader's favour, which alone would legitimize their position. Moreover, since all authority in the party was conferred on particular individuals rather than on offices, it had to be continually confirmed to remain valid. This in turn put pressure on individual leaders to prove both their loyalty and their competence. Before 1933, this was assessed in terms of winning members and voters and this tended to be demonstrated, or at any rate claimed, on the basis of the establishment of offices, networks of agents and so on which then recruited support. In other words, one demonstrated one's competence by expanding one's sphere of competence within the organization. Thus, there was a built-in dynamic within the party organization by which each leader endeavoured to expand his own sphere of action in order both to win the approval of the leader and to prove that he already had it.

On coming to power, the party virtually disintegrated into its component parts. These parts migrated like a stream of parasites through the body politic, establishing themselves in particular organs which they then consumed in order to develop their own individual potency. The history of the party after 1933 consists essentially of the desperate, but largely unavailing, attempts by Hess and, above all, Bormann to put the party together again. While Hess plaintively deplored the lack of solidarity within the party, complaining about those party officials who exhibited 'petty jealousy in regarding anyone whose sphere borders on his own as an enemy because he is afraid that his own sphere will be reduced',[2] Bormann endeavoured to establish a powerful central organization in the shape of the Office of the Führer's Deputy/Party Chancellery, for which the political cadre of the party - Gauleiter, district leaders, branch leaders etc. - would provide the field organization to which, in turn, the various other departments and party organizations would be subordinated. Bormann rightly saw the key to achieving this goal in establishing himself as Hitler's right-hand man, thereby concentrating the authority of the Führer in his own hands.

Unfortunately, however, Hitler was never prepared to grant Bormann the authority he sought; in particular, he refused to allow the <u>Gauleiter</u> to be integrated into an effective hierarchy. In any case, the SS remained as a permanent rival to the political organization of the party as the authentic representative of National Socialism.

The gradual penetration into the existing framework of the German state of the style of leadership and the forms of organization developed within the Nazi party before 1933, contributed to the progressive demoralization and disintegration of the state apparatus. Interference in every sphere of government by party agencies, the appointment by Hitler of numerous special commissioners with powers which cut across and eroded those of the established ministries and government bodies at all levels, the securing from Hitler of <u>ad hoc</u> decisions which went against those of the authorities who were officially responsible - all these developments produced a break-down of the system into a series of virtually autonomous agencies acting largely on their own initiative and in fierce competition with one another. In such an administrative chaos the rational planning, coordination and, implementation of policies became increasingly difficult and the role of the civil servant an unenviable one.

Yet, ironically, as Jane Caplan shows, many civil servants - including the old guard Nazi and subsequent Reich Minister of the Interior Wilhelm Frick - had seen the Nazis as a force which, by destroying the pluralist parliamentary democracy of Weimar, would restore to them the position of authority which they had possessed before 1914. It would recreate a 'professional' civil service in which unqualified 'outsiders', appointed for political reasons after 1918, would no longer be permitted to intrude. Their vision of a 'total state' envisaged a strong authoritarian and centralized government in which the civil service would play the key role as the main instrument of power, free from the interference of party caucuses, parliamentary committees, and pressure groups. This would enable them to carry out major objectives such as a reform of the federal system in the direction of a greater centralization, which had long been frustrated by political obstacles.

As Jane Caplan shows, however, the development of government in the Third Reich was not simply a question of an irrational party apparatus undermining a rational state machine. For the civil service schemes were in themselves hardly more rational than those of the party, given their underlying assumption that they, rather than the Nazi party, embodied the unity and best interests of the state. They failed to comprehend that the paternalist role, which they had acquired in the age of absolutism and which had been sustained in a nineteenth century political system governed by notables, was no longer appropriate to the mass democracy of the twentieth century. Moreover, in practical terms too, the scheme for an authoritarian state run by an elite of civil servants, answerable to a Reich field organization under the Reich Ministry of the Interior, was just as much doomed to failure as Bormann's dream of a single Nazi party cadre controlling the state - because of the jealous opposition of Frick's fellow ministers on the one hand and of Hitler and the party on the other.

One of the main problems faced by the regime in defining

relations between party and state was to sort out their respective
roles. The Nazi party leadership claimed a monopoly of 'politics' which
they defined as Menschenführung (literally 'the leadership of men'),
while they wished to confine the state's activities to Verwaltung
(administration) conceived as the routine implementation of decisions
reached by the politicians. Apart from the fact that the assumption of
a sharp distinction between politics as a creative activity on the one
hand and administration as a purely routine function on the other bears
almost no relation to reality, the senior members of the civil service –
men such as Wilhelm Stuckart, a dedicated Nazi and member of the SS –
had no desire to see their functions restricted to routine matters.

In practice, the party's attempts to exercise political
leadership took the form – at the lower levels – of propaganda, largely
under the supervision of the Reich Ministry of Propaganda, of petty
supervision by local block leaders, and of welfare measures of one kind
and another subject to political and ideological criteria. At the top
they consisted of a limited degree of influence over legislation and a
veto over personnel appointments in the civil service. The party's
success in this field, particularly at local level, was limited by the
inadequacy of its personnel which, in turn, was a consequence of its
failure to develop either a clear conception of its role or an effective
organization to perform that role which might have attracted able men.
This failure was, in part, a consequence of the nature of the movement
as it had developed before 1933. It was also, however, the result of
Hitler's belief that the key to transforming Germany's situation was to
improve German morale by inculcating a new mentality rather than by
transforming the economic and social order. It also reflected the
reality that Germany was dominated by well-entrenched elites who could
only be shifted by revolutionary means for which neither the leadership
nor the social basis of the Nazi movement – however radical some of the
rhetoric and however genuine some of the social frustration – were
fundamentally prepared. If the existing functional elites were left in
place then the only way the party could succeed in establishing a
powerful, let alone dominant, role was by linking itself with one or
more of these elites. Of all the party organizations, however, only the
SS succeeded in achieving this and, as a result, in acquiring a powerful
position. It was only during the exceptional circumstances of the war,
and particularly its latter critical phases, that the political
organization of the party managed to establish a really powerful
presence for itself in the country at large.

Before 1933, Nazism had based its main appeal on its promise
to reunite German society, while Hitler himself regarded morale as the
key to national stength. How successful then was the regime in its
attempt to create a new 'national community' and to restore German
morale?

As Ian Kershaw shows, essentially "Nazism painted over rather
than eliminated the divisions within German society". Because of the
diffuse nature of Nazi ideology, however, most people could identify
with certain aspects of it while opposing others. By conveniently
ignoring the racist elements which did not normally affect most Germans,
it was possible to regard Nazism as a vigorous restatement of many
traditional German bourgeois values – in particular, nationalism, which
had long occupied the supreme position in the German middle class

pantheon. For the majority, a combination of gratitude for economic recovery together with support for an initially highly successful foreign policy outweighed hostility to other aspects of the regime, which - except among the religious, and a small minority with strong political or moral convictions - did not affect people's deepest concerns. Above all, the regime was successful both in identifying its successes with Hitler's leadership and, at the same time, in disassociating the Führer from its negative aspects. In consequence, Hitler provided the crucial integrating and legitimizing force within the regime, enabling it to divert discontent into harmless grumbling about the party funtionaries at local level.

Nevertheless, widespread disaffection with the regime did exist at various times. There was, for example, considerable economic discontent springing from the disillusionment of many of its early supporters among the Mittelstand (petty bourgeoisie) who were adversely affected by the priorities of the rearmament programme. Agriculture, in particular, was seriously affected by the flight from the land to better pay and conditions in the cities which greatly increased the burden on the women who remained behind. Equally, the religious denominations reacted strongly to measures aimed at the Churches. However these discontents among various groups were different from each other. Moreover, the fact that the regime had destroyed rival political parties and prevented the formation of new ones meant that there was no organization which could aggregate these discontents and mount a broad critique of the system. By incorporating the fragmentation of German society into the very structure of the regime itself Nazism compartmentalized and thereby neutralized opinion, while creating in the shape of the Führer a symbolic focus of national unity with which the regime had become identified.

One of the main objectives of those who established the Nazi party had been to win over the working class. The very name of the party - The National Socialist German Workers' Party - represented a programme in itself. It sprang from the belief of those on the racist Right of German politics that the working class had been seduced into supporting internationalist and pacifist doctrines by Jewish socialist agitators and that before Germany could regain her rightful place in the world the working class must be won back for the nation. Thus the response of the working class was crucial to the Nazi attempt to create a new 'national community'.

In his article, Stephen Salter traces the history of the relationship between Nazism and the working class. He shows how, having failed to win over the working class with electoral propaganda before 1933, once in power the Nazis quickly destroyed its representative political and industrial organizations. Demoralized by the effects of the economic crisis and with its organizations split between Communists and Social Democrats, the working class was in a weak position to resist this onslaught of terror. The regime was, however, obliged to fill the vacuum by establishing a new labour organization - the German Labour Front (DAF) - which set up subsidiary sections: 'Strength through Joy' to promote and supervise recreation facilities and 'Beauty of Labour' to press for improved working conditions. Thus, the regime attempted to compensate the working class for the destruction of its independent representative institutions with fringe benefits and a largely rhetorical improvement in status.

For most workers employment was the most vital issue and, as the rearmament boom got under way, not only did full employment soon return, but in those sectors of the economy associated with rearmament labour shortages developed. In consequence, wages rose as employers competed for labour. Moreover, labour exploited its relative scarcity by moving from job to job and by various forms of obstructions such as absenteeism, and even strike action. The regime responded to this situation with a mixture of concession and coercion, reflecting an awareness that the working class had not been won over to the extent of being prepared to tolerate deprivations in order to facilitate an aggressive foreign policy, let alone a war. Significantly, during the course of the war, the element of coercion steadily increased.

These issues are central to a number of important current historical debates on such questions as the domestic context of Hitler's decision to go to war in 1939 and the decision not to conscript women workers during the war. It is beyond the scope of this introduction to deal with these problems, which in any case are very well illuminated by Mr. Salter in his contribution. The important point to note at this stage is his conclusion that the working class were not won over to active identification with the Nazi 'national community' and that this fact had a significant albeit disputed impact on the Nazi regime. The relative quiescence of the working class during the war compared with the First World War is probably the consequence of a combination of much tougher methods of coercion, a marked superiority in living standards through the exploitation of the occupied territories, and, conceivably, the fact that the image of Hitler as a popular leader had some impact even on the working class.

Thus, the Nazi regime failed in its attempt to create a new German 'national community'. Its apparent success at replacing the pluralist system of Weimar with its deep social and ideological fissures by a monolithic unity of 'Ein Reich, ein Volk, ein Führer' was an illusion, a propaganda image. It had been a utopian dream from the start, a product of the inability of the German Right to accept the social consequences of modernization, of its hope that the inevitable conflicts of mass society could somehow be overcome by the rhetoric of national solidarity. Nevertheless, it would be a mistake to deny that, through its appeal to national pride and above all through its success in projecting Hitler as the embodiment of the nation – a success which, of course, would have been impossible without concrete early achievements in the economic and diplomatic fields – for a long time the regime did secure a large measure of support, particularly among the middle and lower middle classes. Above all, however, through its manipulation of traditional German values – patriotism, a military-bureaucratic sense of duty empty of genuine moral content, and deference to established authority – by crushing the organizations of the Left, and by initially pursuing policies which coincided with their interests and aspirations, it succeeded in winning the support of the traditional elites. It was the continued cooperation of the army, the bureaucracy, and industry which enabled the regime to achieve its striking successes.

As time went on, these successes, however spectacular, were

increasingly vitiated by the fact that they were not geared to a set of rationally ordered objectives. Each occurred as if in a vacuum, unrelated to one another, and not integrated into any overall system of priorities. There was a growing lack of co-ordination, a progressive breakdown of communication, an absence of feedback between the different sectors of the system. As a result, those operating the system - men like the Armaments Minister, Albert Speer - increasingly lost touch with reality.[3] They became the victims of a tunnel vision in which they saw only the immediate task ahead; they were oblivious of the wider implications of what they were doing and ignorant - sometimes intentionally - of what other parts of the system were doing. Moreover, the original ideological impetus, which had meanwhile dehumanized opponents through the constant repetition of stereotypes, had been largely superceded as the motor of action by a bureaucratic momentum sustained by the competition for power between the various apparats. In this system the same criteria of bureaucratic efficiency were applied to the murder of millions of Jews as to the manufacture of munitions and personal responsibility had been narrowed to the performance of one's duty (Dienst) within a particular apparatus. The mentality of men like Eichmann, who actually organized and carried out the Final Solution,, was closer to that of Speer than to that of ideological fanatics like Gauleiter Julius Streicher.

The need to maintain the illusion of national harmony not only vis-à-vis outsiders but also themselves, the refusal to accept that social conflict is inevitable prevented the Nazi leadership from developing mechanisms for adjusting sectional divisions and conflict and arriving at a genuine national consensus. Instead, an ersatz form of national unity, a lowest common denominator, was manufactured by provoking conflict with Germany's neighbours. Finally, the fact that Hitler - the embodiment of the national will - proved himself both unwilling and incapable of providing the necessary coordination and direction in home affairs enable, indeed encouraged his lieutenants to indulge in their own private enterprise. In an atmosphere of intense mutual suspicion and hostility they each built up their bureaucratic empires, seeking to win a monopoly of particular functions and to harness particular interests in the pursuit of power for themselves and their clienteles. The state itself became the booty to be carved up between them. The politics of plunder associated with the activities of the Nazi regime outside Germany, merely represented the application abroad of its own domestic form of politics, a politics which had its origins in the struggle for power before 1933. This exploitation of the occupied territories helped to sustain a system which was consuming its substance at an alarming rate. It is questionable, however, how far one can speak of an imminent breakdown through internal stresses. A highly developed sense of social discipline, of duty and service, and a strong patriotism, when combined with an effective system of repression were powerful forces making for stability. Nevertheless, the degree of irrationality, lack of coherence, and friction built into the system was responsible for a wastage of energy, a deterioration in efficiency, and, perhaps above all, a loss of morale on the part of those involved in running the system which boded ill for the future.

Notes

1.   T.W. Mason, <u>Sozialpolitik im Dritten Reich. Arbeiterklasse und Volksgemeinschaft</u> (Opladen, 1977), p.26
2.   Stellvertreter des Führers Verfugung 121/35 14.6.1935 BA NS 6/219
3.   For a devastating critique of Speer's armaments 'miracle' see K.H. Ludwig, <u>Technik und Ingenieure im Dritten Reich</u> (Dusseldorf, 1974)

1. The Nazi Party and the Third Reich: the Myth and Reality of the One-Party State

JEREMY NOAKES

On 30 January 1933, it appeared as if the Nazi party had come into its own. After repeated disappointments Hitler had at last become Reich Chancellor. During the spring and early summer of 1933, Nazi leaders pressed forward to take over positions of authority at all levels. By the beginning of July, all the other political parties had succumbed to intimidation and the erosion of support and had dissolved themselves where they had not already been formally banned. The field was already clear when, in a law dated 14 July, the Nazi party was declared to be the only authorized party and Germany officially became a one party state.

Yet despite the efforts of party zealots headed by Martin Bormann to turn the German one-party state into one in which the party had an effective power and control akin to that of the Bolsheviks in Russia, the Nazi party in Germany failed to exploit to the full the power which had seemingly now come its way. Although leading members secured powerful posts, the party cadre never dominated the administration of the Third Reich. Indeed, as late as the summer of 1941, the Gauleiter of Swabia suggested to Hitler that all the lower ranking party leaders should be drafted to the Russian front for the few months envisaged for the campaign, so insignificant did the function of the party cadre seem.[1] A year later, the Gauleiter of Weser-Ems confessed that 'one day the party will certainly be an elite of leaders, but it is not one yet.'[2] This article will examine why the party's political bureaucracy - its political organization or PO in Nazi parlance - failed to establish itself more effectively within the regime.[3]

1. The Party and the Struggle for Power: the legacy of a conglomerate organization.

Clearly an important factor in the difference in the relative success of the Bolshevik and Nazi parties in establishing themselves within their respective regimes was the political environment in which they were operating. While the Bolshevik party was faced with what was virtually a political and administrative vacuum, the Nazi party found itself confronted with a powerful state machine and entrenched functional elites, including a self-confident bureaucracy with deep historical roots in German politics and society. But equally important was the fact that they were two very different kinds of organization and this difference derived to a large extent from their very different origins. Many of the difficulties of the Nazi party were the result of the way in which it had developed during its early years. It entered the Third Reich with a legacy of organization, function, and personnel which severely limited its ability to adapt to changing conditions after 1933 and to find an appropriate role in the new order.

The party's basic organization had been created by Hitler on its refounding in 1925 after his release from imprisonment for the abortive Munich putsch. He found that his following had spread beyond the borders of Bavaria and was growing fast throughout Germany. To assert his authority over these new members and branches he both set up a party headquarters in Munich, staffed by a few officials who concentrated initially on centralizing control over the issuing of membership cards and collecting membership dues, and also established a direct relationship with the regional leaders or Gauleiter. From the start, therefore, a dichotomy emerged in the party organization which was to prevent it from becoming a united body, and fragmentation increased in the ensuing years.

(a) The relationship between Hitler and the Gauleiter

In 1925 the party outside Munich was already in the hands of the Gauleiter. Most of them were fanatical racists, ambitious and often stubborn men whose primary loyalty was to Hitler. Many had not been members of the Nazi party before and had joined in 1925 along with their followers because they were attracted by Hitler's radical leadership. They were unenthusiastic about what they saw as the attempts of the central party bureaucracy to interfere in the running of the party in what they tended to regard as their own territories. Hitler needed the support of these men in order to establish an effective national organization. On the other hand, they needed his official recognition as Gauleiter in order to legitimize themselves in the eyes of the local Nazis vis-à-vis rivals for the leadership of their areas, a leadership that was often hotly contested during these early years. By about the middle of 1926, Hitler had succeeded in asserting his absolute control over the Gauleiter and, henceforward, he regarded them as his key agents in the field, making them directly responsbile to him for all political activities in their Gaue. Thus these Gauleiter were now answerable both to the central party apparatus and to their leader directly.

Up until about 1928, the Gauleiter were able to assert their authority without too great interference from party headquarters. During this period, their main problem arose from the activities of the party's paramilitary style organizations - the SA and SS - who had yet another chain of command to the leader completely separate from that of the political organization, and who tended, therefore, to assert their independence of the political leadership. From 1928 onwards, however, the position of the Gauleiter and of the PO was increasingly undermined by drastic changes in the membership and organization, changes which were part of the transformation of the party from a political sect of fanatical anti-Semites into a mass movement with a much broader basis of support.

(b) <u>The growth of separate 'interest' sections affiliated to the</u>
<u>party</u>

With the onset of the slump, which began in the agrarian
sector in 1928, the progressive fragmentation of German politics during
the 1920s had begun to accelerate as each group fought for its own
interest in an atmosphere of increasing bitterness and violence. This
disintegration of the body politic, reflecting a wider dissolution of
the social order itself, offered a unique opportunity to a new movement
untainted by the previous system to reintegrate German society and
German politics into a new framework. The Nazi party seized this
opportunity with both hands. Like other parties, only more intensively,
it began to establish a number of separate sections and so-called
affiliated organizations which were geared to winning the support of
various economic and social groups. Some, such as the Hitler Youth,
already existed, but from about 1928 onwards separate sections
mushroomed representing particular professional and economic interests
e.g. for teachers, lawyers, farmers, civil servants, blue and white
collar workers. These groups then played an important role in
facilitating the party's rise to power.

However, although the party succeeded in infiltrating and, in
some cases, even conquering many interest groups, at the same time the
reverse was equally true: interest groups had, in effect, succeeded in
colonizing the party. In the process, they had gone a long way towards
introducing the fragmentation of German society into the party itself.
The <u>Gauleiter</u>, who were obliged to establish branches of these
affiliates in their <u>Gaue</u> were soon complaining in the words of the
<u>Gauleiter</u> of Magdeburg-Anhalt that 'the decentralization into hundreds
of special organizations is ultimately going to split up the whole
party' while 'the <u>Gauleiter</u>...ends up as the propagandist and the man
who collects the membership dues.'[4]

The formation of these specialist organizations offers an
important insight into the development of the Nazi party, for they were
almost invariably founded not by the party headquarters, but by
individuals in various parts of the Reich - the teachers' organization
by Hans Schemm, a teacher from Bayreuth, the civil servants' league by
Jakob Sprenger, a post office clerk from Frankfurt am Main, the lawyers'
organization by Hans Frank, a Munich lawyer, and the agricultural
department by R. W. Darré, an agriculturalist who had returned from the
German colonies after the war, etc. These individuals then persuaded
the party HQ in Munich to give their organizations official recognition,
whereupon they quickly developed centralised bureaucracies of their own.
In other words, to a large extent these affiliates represented a kind of
private enterprise on the part of their founders, who exploited them to
increase their influence within the party and, from then onwards, often
linked their own personal ambitions to the success of the particular
interest group with which they were now associated and to which, in
fact, they usually already belonged. They tended to regard these
affiliates as their own private empires as much as party organizations.

GPPNG - B

(c) <u>The growth of functional empires within the expanding party</u>

This fragmentation within the party was, however, not only a result of the multiplication of the affiliated organizations. The increasing size of the party encouraged greater functional specialisation. For example, after his appointment as the party's propaganda chief in 1929, Joseph Goebbels expanded the propaganda department until there was soon an elaborate vertical propaganda apparatus with separate departments at <u>Gau</u>, <u>Kreis</u> (district), and local levels, which from now onwards were bombarded with a constant stream of circulars and directives from the propaganda headquarters in Munich. This elaborate and highly centralized propaganda apparatus had the advantage of providing effective co-ordination for the party's propaganda campaigns, but at the same time, it introduced yet another vertical structure and, what is more, removed from the political leaders – <u>Gauleiter</u>, <u>Kreisleiter</u> and local branch leaders – control over what had hitherto been their main function – namely propaganda. <u>Gauleiter</u> Kube of <u>Gau</u> Ostmark complained in December 1930 that 'the position of a <u>Gauleiter</u> is becoming more and more undignified. The tone adopted by the Reich propaganda headquarters is liable to persuade the <u>Gauleiter</u> to give up their positions...'[5]

(d) <u>Gregor Strasser's failure to establish party centralization</u>

The party headquarters was aware of these dangers. Gregor Strasser, the organization chief, intended that the <u>Gauleiter</u> should perform a coordinating role at regional level among the various party sections. However, in return for supporting the <u>Gauleiter</u> and the cadre vis-à-vis the specialist sections and affiliated groups, Strasser expected the <u>Gauleiter</u> to regard themselves as subordinate functionaries of party headquarters. Indeed, between 1928 and 1932, Strasser endeavoured to introduce an altogether more rational hierarchical structure. Such attempts, however, went against the grain of the party. For, although the enormous growth in the membership had obliged Hitler to institutionalize his charisma in a more and more elaborate organization, he had no intention of allowing himself to be shackled by Strasser's bureaucratic structures. He had personally appointed or confirmed both the heads of the departments and affiliated sections as well as the <u>Gauleiter</u>, and he regarded them all as his agents, underlining this by his practice of dealing with them directly rather than through Strasser and the party headquarters. Just as important, they regarded Hitler as their immediate superior and considered themselves, as Hitler's agents, to be the equals of the other members of the headquarters staff, including Strasser. Not surprisingly therefore, when Gregor Strasser resigned from the party in December 1932, Hitler seized the opportunity to break up the potentially powerful central apparatus into three separate components . Moreover, he now insisted that the position of the <u>Gauleiter</u> – his 'most important representatives' within the party – should be 'as sovereign as possible.'[6]

(e) A fragmented structure.

On the threshold of power, then, the Nazi party was
essentially a conglomeration of apparats representing particular
interests - professional, occupational, and social, together with a
paramilitary organization which in turn was split into two, with one
group (the SS) by now only nominally subordinate to the other (the SA).
This conglomeration was loosely tied to a cadre political organization
whose main function was propaganda and whose main bases of power were
regional - the Gaue. This regional bias had just received an added
impetus with the break-up of Strasser's central party apparatus. In a
very real sense there were now 32 Nazi parties, one for each Gau.

These various party organizations were led by a group of
political entrepreneurs. The party was in the business of political
mobilization, using propaganda to win members and voters as the key to
power. In a situation in which it was not always clear who was using
whom, each of these individual leaders harnessed behind their particular
organizations the hopes, fears, interests, aspirations, and resentments
of various economic and social groups. These ambitious individuals and
disparate groups were held together by the hope of power - intending to
carve out a stake in the future regime either territorially as a
Gauleiter or functionally and organizationally as a leader of one of the
numerous party agencies - SA, Hitler Youth, propaganda, agriculture etc.
They were united by a strong, emotionally charged, conviction that
Hitler's leadership offered the best chance of achieving power and by a
sense of comradeship derived from membership of a movement which was at
odds with the rest of society and yet rationalized its hunger for power
and for the satisfaction of its grievances with the - sometimes
sincerely held - conviction that it had a mission to transform Germany's
fortunes and restore her to greatness.

2. The Party and the Take-Over of Power: Problems of Adaptation
    and Coordination.

After the take-over of power at all levels during the first
few months of 1933, the Nazi party found itself facing a crisis of
identity. It had been geared above all to the acquisition of power; it
had made few preparations for the exercise of power. In the absence of
a strong central apparatus to provide effective coordination, the latent
fragmentation of the movement now became actual and the party began to
disintegrate into its component parts.

(a) The specialist sections seek autonomy.

In a process which played a key role in the Nazi take-over of
power, the various specialist sections and departments - often acting
more or less autonomously - proceeded to take-over or 'coordinate'
existing public and private organizations in their particular fields and
to establish themselves as official or quasi-official bodies. As such
they simultaneously represented and controlled various occupational and
social groups and performed particular functions for the regime. In
some cases, as with the party's agrarian department and the propaganda
department, they were in effect subordinated to official government
bodies through the personal union of state and party offices in the

hands of their chiefs - the Reich Minister of Agriculture, Walther
Darré, and the Reich Minister of Propaganda, Joseph Goebbels. Even
where this did not occur - as, for example, with the Nazi Teachers'
League - there was a tendency for such agencies to seek to emancipate
themselves from the political organization (PO) by establishing large
bureaucracies of their own. In theory, all these organizations remained
linked to the party as so-called 'party formations' (SA, SS, Hitler
Youth), 'affiliated associations' (e.g. German Labour Front, NS-League
of Teachers, NS-People's Welfare) or organizations under the supervision
of the party' (e.g. German Students' Association, German Local
Government Association). However, the extent and nature of these links
varied greatly. In particular the SA and, after July 1934, the SS, in
theory 'party formations', had in fact become completely independent
empires.

(b) <u>State office versus party office</u>.

The seizure of power produced other centrifugal pressures
operating within the party. The first few months of 1933 saw the
take-over of official posts by leaders of the PO at all levels. Not
only did they take over most of the ministries in the federal states
but, lower down the scale, by 1 January 1935, of 827 Nazi district
leaders (<u>Kreisleiter</u>) 69 had become <u>Landräte</u> (district governors), 150
<u>Oberbürgermeister</u> (lord mayors), and 37 <u>Bürgermeister</u> (mayors).
Finally, 3,963 local branch or 'base' (<u>Stützpunkt</u>) leaders were now
<u>Bürgermeister</u> or parish council chairmen.[7] There was clearly a danger
of the party being simply absorbed into the state and local government
with party leaders at all levels being attracted by the status,
salaries, and security offered by government posts. There was a strong
tendency for those Nazi leaders who acquired state or municipal posts
increasingly to disengage themselves from the party, a process
encouraged by the fact that many of those in senior posts were more
highly qualified than the majority of their comrades. These men did not
cease to be 'Nazi', but they believed that Nazi goals, as they
understood them, could be best achieved through a 'coordinated' state
machine rather than through the party apparatus which lacked the
necessary expertise. Indeed, they increasingly came to resent party
interference in their new spheres of responsibility and advocated the
restriction of the party to purely propaganda functions.

As part of this same process, and in the absence of an
effective central party apparatus, the <u>Gauleiter</u> were liable to become
independent barons, entrenched in their regional fiefs and tolerating no
authority other than Hitler himself. In July 1933, for example, it was
reported that <u>Gauleiter</u> Erich Koch of East Prussia had announced to a
meeting of 150 of his party officials: 'Who cares about Berlin, here in
East Prussia I'm the one who gives the orders!'[8] This problem was
compounded by the fact that all but nine of the thirty-two <u>Gauleiter</u> had
also acquired senior state offices either as <u>Reichsstatthalter</u> (governor
of a <u>Land</u>) <u>Oberpräsident</u> (governor of a Prussian province), or (in
Bavaria) as <u>Minister</u> or <u>Regierungspräsident</u> (governor of a county).
They did not, however, fall victim to the process of disengagement from
the party which had afflicted other members of the party who had
acquired state posts. This was partly because at any rate until the war
- their state functions remained largely honorific. As a result, in

order to retain and expand their power, they were obliged to emphasize
the legitimation derived from their party role. More particularly, the
vast majority of them had few administrative skills and even less
inclination to move in that direction. Most were, like their Führer,
propagandists first and last with a profound dislike not simply of the
limitations imposed by legal and administrative processes but of the
whole mentality of the bureaucracy.

(c) The party in limbo.

        With the capture of the German state, with the partial or
complete emancipation of many of its various specialist formations and,
in particular, with its main responsibility for propaganda removed to
the new Propaganda Ministry, the party's cadre organization (PO) was in
danger of being left as a rump without any kind of raison d'être, of
being relegated to a limbo by the - in theory - Nazified state machine,
and of disintegrating into its Gau components. The central issue was
the question of what role the PO should play now that Hitler had
achieved supreme power over the highly efficient German bureaucracy.
This in turn raised the question of how the party should be organized to
fulfil that role and, in particular, what should be its relationship
with the state. Finally, there was the question of how the population
would respond to this role.

3. The Führer and the Party: 'Hitler Party' or a 'Nazi Party'?

(a) Hitler's view of the function of the party in the Third
     Reich.

        As far as Hitler was concerned, the main role of the party
was to prepare the German people psychologically for war. Ideally, this
involved creating a new mentality by indoctrinating them with Nazi
ideology - in particular with its racist and social-darwinist
imperatives and the absolute priority which it gave to national
interests and goals, as defined by the Führer, over the concerns of the
individual citizen. Hitler was aware that this would take time - time
which he lacked. Meanwhile, therefore, in practice he envisaged the
party fulfilling two major roles. Firstly, it would assume
responsibility for the morale of the German people, mobilizing them in
support of the regime and its measures. As he told the Party Congress
in September 1934: the party must be 'continually educating - and above
all supervising - the nation...so that no reverse let alone a decline
occurs. [For,] we do not intend to suffer the fate of that world which
was replaced in 1918' - that is revolution.[9] Arguably, this role
might have been achieved most effectively by transforming the PO into a
field agency of the Propaganda Ministry, as some advocated. Such a move
was, however, precluded for a number of reasons. It would have
alienated a large group of fanatically loyal supporters. As he told his
military adjutant in September 1938, the leaders of the PO 'would all
jump with a parachute if he ordered them to. For they had faith,
whereas the Army generals did not.'[10] Also it would have weakened his
position vis-à-vis the existing power groups, notably the civil service.
Indeed, the second main role which he envisaged for the party was as a

kind of watchdog over and goad for the civil service to ensure that it did not act as a brake on his policies and, where necessary, to take over the execution of measures which the civil service proved unwilling or incapable of implementing. Hitler felt precluded from carrying out a radical purge of the civil service because he was unwilling to jeopordize the delicate compromise with the traditonal German elites on which the regime - initially at any rate - was based; he was also unwilling to risk disrupting the major priorities of a return to full employment and the inauguration of a big rearmament programme, particularly since these elites were clearly prepared to cooperate with the new order in the pursuit of goals which they considered to coincide with their own. On the other hand, however, he was profoundly suspicious of what he saw as the conservative, immobile, and legalistic nature of the civil service.

Hitler sought to mobilize the German people and looked to the party to proved the dynamic impetus, untrammeled by legal or moral inhibitions, which was vital if he was to achieve his wider goals. The problem was how to devise a relationship between party and state which would combine the administrative efficiency characteristic of the state with the ideological fanaticism and political dynamism of the party. It was like an attempt to square a circle. However, before he could hope to use the party as an effective organization, let alone devise a framework for its relationship with the state, he had to preserve it from totally disintegrating into its component parts - a very real threat in the spring of 1933.

(b) Hitler and the party organization.

How far Hitler was aware of this danger is not clear. At this time, his main attention was focused on affairs of state and he seems to have wished to avoid being drawn into the growing conflicts between the various party organizations as they fought over spheres of jurisdiction. It was probably mainly for this reason that, on 21 April 1933, he appointed his private secretary, Rudolf Hess, who was already head of the Party Central Commission (one of the three remaining components of Strasser's old central apparatus), to the new post of the Führer's Deputy for Party Affairs (St.d.F.). Hess was a totally loyal and relatively unambitious figure who could be expected to be an acceptable arbiter of party disputes. Clearly, once having been appointed to such a position Hess found himself compelled to defend it. It is doubtful, however, whether he would have succeeded in making much of the new office had he not appointed as his chief of staff an exceptionally able young bureaucrat from the party treasurer's office, Martin Bormann, who immediately set about building up the 'staff of the Führer's Deputy'. It was Bormann's (and Hess's) aim to assert the claim of his office to supreme authority within the party and, in particular, to monopolize the party's relations with the agencies of the state.

By the end of 1935, the core of the St.d.F.'s office consisted of two main departments: - Department II for Party Affairs and Department III for State Affairs. Within these departments Bormann established desks covering a growing range of areas of policy - culture, economics, technology, legal affairs etc. - each of which ultimately implied a claim to supreme jurisdiction in that particular sphere.

Department III was staffed with civil servants, known to be loyal party members, who were seconded from government departments at Bormann's request. Its authority was based primarily on two Führer decrees of 1934 and 1935 which gave the St.d.F. the right to participate at all stages in the drafting of government bills and regulations and laid down that the St.d.F. must approve the appointment and promotion of all civil servants of any importance. These were both weapons of considerable potential and there is no doubt that, from a very early stage, Bormann intended through his office to establish a dominant role for the party vis-à-vis the state. Thus, he wrote to the Nazi Reich Minister of the Interior on 26 May 1935: 'It is the function of the party to create the will of the state' - a somewhat opaque statement which, however, left room for the broadest possible interpretation of the party's role.[11] The function of the state, on the other hand, was 'to administer'. In fact, the relationship between the party and the civil service became more one of constant interference than of systematic control, with the party becoming more adept at negative delaying tactics than at developing positive initiatives.

One reason for this was the fact that the party never succeeded in breaking down separatist tendencies and establishing itself as a really effective organization. This became the task of Department II of the St.d.F.'s office under its head, Hellmuth Friedrichs. Bormann and Friedrichs aimed to turn the party into a hierarchical structure in which the PO would form the basic territorial cadre organization to which as many as possible of the party formations and affiliates should be subordinated at each level. This certainly represented a rational framework and in many ways it was similar to Gregor Strasser's objective before 1933. Unfortunately, however, as Strasser himself had discovered there were serious obstacles in the way of implementing it.

The main problem was the fact that Hitler was not prepared to allow the St.d.F. and his office to acquire a monopoly of central authority within the party. Why is not entirely clear. It may be that Hitler was not particularly interested in the party and was also not anxious to antagonize old comrades by intervening to restrict their fields of competence. Arguably, he preferred to let matters take their course, leaving individual party leaders to fight it out among themselves. This would also have conformed with his social darwinist view of the benefits of struggle in producing the best results. It could also, however, have been a more conscious policy of 'divide and rule' leaving himself the maximum freedom of manoeuvre. There are in fact good grounds for thinking that he acted more from an instinctive unwillingness to allow his hands to be tied by the emergence of too strong a party organization, an instinct which would have been reinforced by his experience of Gregor Strasser's 'betrayal'. The more lines which led directly to himself, the less danger there would be to his position. He had always regarded the party as essentially a 'Hitler party' rather than a Nazi party and such was his charismatic appeal to the membership that he had succeeded in imposing this view on the party. His popular appeal was of course the party's greatest strength but, at the same time, the charismatic nature of the movement was to prove its greatest weakness in the sense that it prevented the centralization of the party and the formation of an effective rationally-structured organization.

Thus, while in theory the St.d.F.'s office was responsible for laying down the political guidelines for the party, in practice it continued to be faced with competing agencies at the highest level in the party who were not invariably disposed to accept its jurisdiction. For example, the party treasurer, Franz Schwarz, had a vertical organization of officials reporting directly to him and jealously guarded his control over the party's finances for which he was responsible only to Hitler. Moreover, Schwarz was only the most independent of the heads of the various specialist party offices – local government, youth, culture etc. – all of whom considered themselves both directly answerable to Hitler and also the superiors of the political officials as far as their own particular sphere was concerned. Furthermore, this position appeared to be underlined by Hitler himself when, on 2 June 1933, he appointed sixteen of these departmental heads as Reichsleiter, a title which meant nothing in terms of additional powers but which undoubtedly represented a significant boost to their self-esteem and to their individual status within the regime. In the face of this situation, the St.d.F.'s office had a tough struggle to assert their authority over the Reichsleiter. It was Bormann's and Friedrichs' ambition to absorb the functions of the various semi-autonomous party departments into their own office and to this end they created parallel specialist sections within Department II. However, it was not really until the pressures of conscription and material shortages arose during the critical phase of the war that they were able to close down some of these departments.

An even more serious obstacle than the Reichsleiter was that represented by the so-called 'Chief of staff of the PO' (from 1934 known as the Reich Organization Leader), Robert Ley, who had inherited most of Gregor Strasser's responsibilities. On 20 December 1932, Hitler had announced that Ley would deputize for him as 'supreme head of the whole political party apparatus and of all leaders of the movement' – with the exception of the Gauleiter, who were to remain directly subordinate to the Führer.[12] In practice, this meant that Ley was responsible for matters of personnel, organization, and training. Moreover, Ley also controlled a number of affiliates, notably the DAF which, with its huge membership and its enormous financial resources from subscriptions and from the confiscated funds of the Trade Unions, represented a major power factor in the regime. The next few years were to see a constant struggle between Hess and Bormann on the one hand and Ley on the other for control over the party, a struggle in which the staff of the St.d.F. slowly but inexorably gained the advantage. Their success owed much to the fact that Bormann not only progressively supplanted Hess in the role of Hitler's secretary but, above all, proved much more successful at converting constant proximity to the Führer into real political influence – particularly while Hitler was preoccupied with running the war. In other words, by placing himself in front of Hitler and acting as his mouthpiece, Bormann gathered more and more of the lines into his own hands in an attempt to turn the Hitler party into a Nazi party by using Hitler's own authority.

4. The Party in the Third Reich: the Attempt to establish an
    effective Hierarchy and a Role.

(a) Efforts to subordinate the Gauleiter to the St.d.F.'s
     office.

        The efforts of Department II of the St.d.F.'s office to
assert its authority within the party proved arduous and time-consuming.
Although Hess and Bormann were gradually able to increase their
authority within the PO at the expense of Ley, the fact that during the
1930s the party contained what were, in effect, two central offices
vying for control not only helped preserve a measure of independence for
Reichsleiter such as Alfred Rosenberg with his various pseudo-cultural
organizations, but also helped to sustain the autonomy of the Gauleiter.
The Gauleiter, in particular proved a formidable obstacle in the way of
the establishment of an effective party hierarchy, for their assertion
of independence was bolstered by Hitler who reiterated on a number of
occasions, the last of which was as late as February 1944, that the
Gauleiter were directly responsible to him.[13] Moreover, in the
process of building up the party organization in their particular areas,
they had been able to establish cliques of loyal supporters within the
Gau party apparatus on whose loyalty they could rely.

        The staff of the St.d.F. endeavoured to overcome the
entrenched local power bases of the Gauleiter in a number of ways. One
method was to attempt to bypass them by establishing close links with
the Gau chiefs of staff (Stabsamtsleiter), who frequently bore much of
the burden of party administration as the Gauleiter themselves
increasingly opted out in order to concentrate on trying to expand their
governmental responsibilities, or on business activities, alcohol, and
other private pleasures. They also sought direct contact with the
district leaders (Kreisleiter), who became increasingly important
figures within the apparatus because the party districts coincided with
those of the state authorities and thus it was at this level that party
and state tended to come closest into contact. To strengthen these
links, a scheme was introduced in 1935 whereby provincial party
officials were seconded to Munich for tours in the Brown House with the
idea that they would then return to their Gaue as, in effect, agents of
the St.d.F. Also, when a vacancy occurred through the death or
dismissal of a Gauleiter, the opportunity was taken to try and secure
the appointment of a man who was acceptable to the St.d.F. The
intention clearly was eventually to replace most of the pre-1933
Gauleiter with party officials who would be loyal subordinates of the
Munich headquarters fitting into their place within the hierarchy.

        The problem was, however, that the numbers involved in this
training programme were small and so this process would take time.
Meanwhile, Bormann and his colleagues were stuck with the existing
Gauleiter. As Bormann himself noted in 1939: 'I know that the 41
Gauleiter are not all perfect, but one simply has to accept the
weaknesses which unfortunately exist in those who at present occupy this
high rank in order to ensure: 1. that the other Gauleiter remain secure
and 2. to make the position of Gauleiter appear impregnable to the
outside world.'[14] Otherwise, he went on, opponents of the PO would
'certainly make an attempt to bring down the Gauleiter by demonstrating

the existence of defects.' This last sentence indicates that relations between the St.d.F. and the <u>Gauleiter</u> were not simply antagonistic but also reflected common interests. On the one hand, the St.d.F. had an interest in building up the <u>Gauleiter</u> as the key officers of its field administration to enable it to impose its authority in the provinces both on the agencies of the state and on those of rival Nazi organizations of whom the SS represented the most ominous threat for the future. On the other hand, the <u>Gauleiter</u> themselves could benefit from a strong St.d.F. to defend the position of the PO at national level against the state and other Nazi agencies.

Part of Bormann's policy of building up the <u>Gauleiter</u> was to discourage the combination of both state and party offices which had occurred in a considerable number of cases in the wake of the Nazi take-over. He considered this separation essential if the PO was to hold together as a cadre and avoid the danger of being eclipsed by the state agencies on the one hand and the party affiliates on the other. Under an order of 19 February 1937, therefore, all district and branch leaders who simultaneously held a state or municipal office were obliged to choose by 1 October which of the two offices – party or state – they wished to retain and to renounce the other. It was a good indication of the weakness of the party that a large number preferred to retain their state or municipal positions.

(b) <u>The party organization's view of the party's role.</u>

What then did the staff of the St.d.F. see as the function of the party? The standard formula used by party leaders at all levels to describe its role was the term <u>Menschenführung</u> (literally 'the leadership of people'). This was a concept so nebulous and all-embracing as to justify the assumption of responsibility by the party for anything which could be considered to affect the lives of the German people, and this was certainly how Bormann wished it to be understood. In practice, it implied a concern with matters which affected public morale and also with the enforcement of basic principles of Nazi ideology, notably anti-Semitism. This was a role for which the leaders of the PO felt themselves peculiarly well-suited. By comparison with the state authorities who were seen as pen-pushers, governed by rules and regulations, they believed that they were uniquely qualified to feel the pulse of the nation and to guide it in the right direction. This was a self-confidence acquired from the pre-1933 period. These men had begun as propagandists whose main aim was to convert the German people to Nazism, to win members and voters, and most of them remained propagandists to the end. In their own estimation they had 'conquered' their particular area for Hitler – they had 'saved' the nation from the abyss of Bolshevism and Jewish domination and had restored national unity and pride. They now felt their prime responsibility was to ensure that the people in their particular area did not waver in their loyalty to the new order. Moreover, they were aware that this was how the <u>Führer</u> assessed their performance. This often placed them in an awkward position. On the one hand, it was their responsibility to 'sell' unpopular measures; price increases, tax increases, shortages, and so on; on the other hand, the unpopularity of such measures often prompted them to protest to the government agencies responsible, protests to which Hitler in particular tended to be sensitive.

In order to carry out the task of Menschenführung effectively the party came to the conclusion that it was essential to impose close supervision on as many aspects of people's lives as possible. So partly as a substitute for its traditional role of propaganda, which had been lost to Goebbels' propaganda ministry, the party evolved the concept of Betreuung to describe one form of the practical application of the idea of Menschenführung. The word Betreuung combines the sense of the words 'care for' and 'supervise', with the implication that those being cared for are incapable of looking after themselves. The adoption of such an all-embracing role, combining welfare and indoctrination duties, had important implications for the organization of the party. Since it involved a much closer involvement in other people's lives, it required a much larger number of party agents at grass roots level. This change in the emphasis of the party's activities from propaganda to Betreuung was reflected in the reform of the party's organization at the bottom levels carried out in 1936. The existence of branches, cells, and blocks was no longer determined by the number of party members in a particular area but on the number of households. Henceforward, a local branch contained no more than 1,500 households divided into cells of four to five blocks. The blocks, which contained 40-60 households (c.160-240 people) were the primary unit of the party organization. They were run by block leaders assisted by house wardens or block helpers in charge of houses or blocks of flats. To fulfill this new role the number of branch leaders increased from 1 January 1935 - 1 January 1939 from 20,724 to 28,376, the number of cell leaders from 54,976 to 89,378, and the number of block leaders from 204,359 to 463,048.[15] The success of the party in its chosen role of Menschenführung depended not only on the effectiveness of its organization at the top - the ability of the St.d.F. to impose his central authority over rival party agencies - and on the establishment of an effective hierarchy in the field, but also and above all on the quality and morale of these subordinate leaders and of the party's rank and file in general. For it was at this level that party and people rubbed shoulders; it was here that Betreuung would be carried out.

The blocks were the primary units of the party organization and the block leaders were the party representatives who came into closest contact with the average citizen; they were obliged to keep a file with the personal details of the inhabitants of their block. The model for the block leader, indeed for the grass roots cadre leadership in general, was a kind of secularised priest or pastor, and the ideal form of Betreuung was outlined in a party memorandum of 1940. After insisting that the PO leader should have cut all ties with the Church, it went on:

> 'he must concern himself with everything in his
> sphere of authority. He must, therefore, find
> out everything that is going on. He must
> intervene everywhere. He will offer
> congratulations on the occasion of births and
> weddings, condolences for deaths; when sickness
> and need are present in a house he will be there;
> he will know the family situation and will be
> concerned with the maintenance of the family...he
> will keep a check on the willingness to
> contribute to collections, participation in

> clubs, the attitude to the party and to the
> church; he will know the political background of
> the family; he will know which families suffer
> from hereditary defects; he will know the
> grumblers and know-alls as well as the reliable
> and loyal ones...He will meet them at work, get
> to know them during collections and propaganda
> actions, will talk to them after work in the
> street or at the pub about the current political
> issues...'[16]

Who then were these local party activists and to what extent did they
measure up to the model?

(c) **The changing nature of the party membership - the
demoralization of the 'old fighters'.**

Hitler's appointment as Chancellor and, in particular, the
election of 5 March 1933 were followed by an enormous influx of new
members into the party. By 1 May over 1.5 million people had applied to
join - an increase of over 150%.[17] Most of these so called 'March
casualties' were opportunists jumping on the bandwagon, including some
250,000 civil servants who were concerned to protect their jobs and
promotion prospects. On the one hand, the party was anxious to recruit
people with the necessary skills to enable it to exert effective
influence in the various spheres of German life, but, on the other hand,
this influx of opportunists threatened to undermine further the already
limited cohesion of the party and to weaken its sense of ideological
commitment. For such recruits tended to be Karteigenossen (comrades on
the files) rather than active Parteigenossen. For this reason, the
files were closed on 1 May 1933. However, a combination of financial
exigency and the urgent need for personnel to undertake Betreuung duties
compelled a 'relaxation' on 1 May 1937 and, two years later, on 1 May
1939, the lifting of all restrictions on entry until February 1942, when
they were reimposed for all except Hitler Youth graduates. By 1935,
with a membership of some 2.5 million, the vast majority of whom were
male (women 5.5%), the party constituted 10.2% of male adults (0.5%
women). By 1943, with 6.5 million male members, this proportion had
risen to 23%. These figures exclude the party formations and affiliates
with, in some cases, a membership many times that of the party itself.
After 1 January 1935, we lack data on the social composition of the
membership, but it probably continued to have a significant bias towards
the middle and lower middle classes who tended to fill occupations where
party membership was more or less compulsory. On 1 January 1935 workers
constituted 30.3% of the party (46.3% of the employed population), white
collar workers 19.4% (12.4%), self-employed 19.6% (9.6%), civil servants
12.4% (4.8%), peasants 10.2% (20.7%), others 3.2% (6.2%).[18]

The dilution of 'old fighters' by the influx of 'March
casualties' added to the difficulties produced by the haemorrhage of
often able party members who had moved into official posts and
henceforward had little time or inclination for party work. Hess, who
acted as a kind of moral tutor to the party, complained that

> 'it makes a very bad impression when comrades who
> have 'got somewhere' now separate themselves off
> from their simple loyal fellow fighters and, in
> order to appear 'socially acceptable', seek an
> entree into circles which have always rejected
> National Socialism.'[19]

Moreover, Hitler's refusal to carry out a major purge of the state
administration or a fundamental reorganization of the economy resulted
in many of these 'simple loyal fellow fighters' becoming disillusioned
by the failure of the regime to fulfill their often highly ambitious
expectations. As the district leader of Hildesheim–Land reported on 13
January 1934:

> 'the old fighters are gradually coming to the
> conclusion that the Nazi revolution has been
> messed up and the previous successes are being
> quietly destroyed. The old fighters are showing
> signs of resignation and an unwillingness to go
> on fighting.'[20]

This apathy springing from disillusionment was then reinforced by an
improvement in the economic situation as the economic boom got under
way. The spontaneous enthusiasm of the pre-1933 members, who had been
responding to a major crisis in their lives, largely evaporated. As a
result, the activities of the party became increasingly bureaucratized
into a ritual of regular 'celebrations' - Hitler's appointment as
Chancellor, May Day in its new form introduced by Goebbels, the Harvest
Festival etc. - of collections for the Winter Aid Programme and other
causes, and periodic membership meetings - enlivened only by the
occasional plebiscite or visit by a V.I.P.

Where they did not lapse into apathy, the 'old fighters'
tended to seek compensation for their failure to benefit more tangibly
from the regime and for their resentment at those who had done so - in
their view unjustly - in a hard-line implementation of Nazi ideological
principles and, where they had the opportunity, the exercise of a petty
tyranny over their fellow citizens. Such actions seemed to reaffirm the
fact that they had triumphed after all. In the absence of ideological
enemies on the Left after the crushing of the Communists, Socialists,
and liberal democrats, and with the ideological enemies on the Right
('Reaction') now in alliance with the Nazi leadership, the Churches, and
above all the Jews, remained as the main targets for the social
frustration of the party cadre. This hard line pressure from the lower
ranks of the party tended to have a 'fly wheel' effect, pushing policy
in a more radical direction as the leadership periodically confirmed
faits accomplis at the bottom through laws and decrees or decided to
unleash this pressure for particular purposes (e.g. Goebbels and the
Reichskristallnacht of November 1938).

(d) Party performance.

Bormann's objective of establishing the PO as a political
elite was frustrated, apart from anything else, by the failure to
attract able recruits. This was largely a consequence of the failure to

work out an effective role for the party. By comparison with the real
power and concrete responsibilities exercised by the SS in the form of
police functions of all kinds, the concept of Menschenführung, with its
as yet limited sphere of effective action, must have appeared
unattractive to ambitious young men. Moreover, the main area of its
practical application in the form of Betreuung came to be concentrated
increasingly in the hands of the party affiliates – notably in the DAF
with its recreation agency, 'Strength Through Joy', and in the Nazi
welfare organization, the NSV. Both of these developed vertical field
administrations parallel to those of the PO and, while in theory they
were subordinate to the party cadre, in practice this subordination was
not always easy to enforce.

As Bormann himself repeatedly pointed out, the proliferation
of bureaucracies both among the affiliates and also among various state
organizations soon produced an acute shortage of suitable candidates for
the PO.[21] This problem was exacerbated by the lack of a proper salary
scale and by often uncompetitive salaries. Salaries within the PO
varied considerably depending on the resources of the individual Gaue.
Party officials at branch level and below were mostly unpaid, but at Gau
and (from 1936) district level there were a considerable number of
full-time paid officials. In general, however, the PO suffered from a
chronic shortage of finance – in sharp contrast to some affiliates.
Unlike the SA, SS, and Hitler Youth, which received a substantial annual
subsidy from the state, until 1938 the PO received no regular funds from
the central government.[22] It was obliged to depend on membership
dues, the sale of party insignia, brochures etc., and on ad hoc
collections and donations from local government. In 1938 the PO was at
last included in the subsidy from the Reich Finance Ministry and, by
1940, it was receiving 59.4 million RM, a sum which increased to 68.5
million in 1941 and 90 million in 1942. This subsidy at last enabled
the party treasurer to introduce a proper salary scale in 1940; but in
the middle of the war it could have little effect on recruitment.

The party's attempts to provide for its own recruitment by
establishing special schools (the Adolf Hitler Schools) and special
colleges (the Ordensburgen) were largely ineffective. The quality of
education at these institutions with its emphasis on physical training
and crude indoctrination produced arrogant and limited young men who
were extremely unpopular even within the party and proved themselves
unsuitable either as 'leaders of men' or as administrators. Many
graduates of the Adolf Hitler Schools did not even take up a career in
the party, preferring business or the military. Similarly, as the
Gauleiter of Dusseldorf pointed out in April 1939, applications to the
Ordensburgen were inadequate because most people in the relevant age
range (21-27 years) had already found themselves careers which evidently
appeared more attractive than the prospects offered by the PO.[23] Nor
could this shortage of career recruits be overcome by unpaid volunteers,
for Gau Dusseldorf alone was some 7-8,000 volunteers short in 1939. The
result was that many of the block leaders were not even members of the
party itself but only of one of its affiliates such as the NSV.

The practical problems of running the party at local level
shortly before the outbreak of war were outlined by the branch leader of
Hachenburg in a rural part of Hesse in a report to his district leader.
After describing the difficulty of holding membership meetings because

of the problem of getting hold of adequate speakers, he went on:

> '...The audience has got smaller and smaller. To
> start with the factory owners, better off
> shopkeepers and the Karteigenossen in general
> stayed away and then the others copy them because
> they see they can get away with it. Nothing
> happens to the others. The party comrades have
> become lazy!!! Many comrades are doing too well
> nowadays, others work flat out and get fed up.
> People often say to me: he is a comrade, earns
> plenty of money, doesn't bother about anything
> and yet is somebody...and the rest of us small
> men are supposed to do the work, which isn't even
> acknowledged.'[24]

A major problem for the PO of the party which is reflected in
this quotation is that, on the whole, it never succeeded in winning
acceptance from the local elites or in establishing itself as an
alternative elite. This was particularly true in areas where there was
a well-entrenched local establishment especially – as was not
infrequently the case in rural districts – if it was both deeply
religious and arch-conservative in outlook. To such people the local
branch or district leader appeared as an upstart trying to usurp their
traditional authority and prestige and a threat to religion. This might
well win the party the support of individuals or sections of the
community who for various reasons resented this dominance of the
traditional hierarchy. For example, in Catholic areas the local school
teacher sometimes continued his traditional battle with the local priest
in Nazi uniform. Such people, however, tended to form the minority.
The traditional deferential mentality remained remarkably resistant to
Nazi egalitarian propaganda, at any rate among the older generation,
and, in any case, the calibre of the local Nazi leadership was not high
enough to provide an attractive elite. While the regime as a whole was
remarkably successful at winning the cooperation of the various elites,
within the Nazi movement as such only the SS had some success in
recruiting substantial numbers from the traditional elites and
integrating them with new men to form a new Nazi elite. As far as the
party itself was concerned, a complaint from an 'old fighter' in Bavaria
from 1944 about the contempt of the local business community was
typical:

> 'as far as they are concerned, the party is
> merely an organization of the poor with which one
> maintains contact only insofar as it is to one's
> advantage to do so...'[25]

Clearly much depended on the quality of the block leaders who
potentially were a very effective instrument of supervision for the
regime. The diplomat, Erich Kordt, wrote after the war that the block
leaders by their

> 'almost complete insight into the private life of
> the individual...and...by their daily,
> matter-of-fact and often unconscious supervision
> of the tenants contributed more to the

strengthening of the regime than did the
Gestapo...It was considerably more difficult to
keep a secret from one's often harmless block
leader - who was, however, obliged to report all
his observations - than to mislead the
Gestapo.'[26]

Although sometimes effective as petty spies, it is clear that
most block leaders fell far short of the pastoral model held up to them.
Thus, the district leader of St. Goarshausen in the Rheingau confessed
in June 1939:

'We have not got the right men for this extremely
important but very difficult task...The majority
are aged, bodily handicapped, and furthermore
intellectually very dull and inactive persons,
[who have] tended to restrict themselves to the
sale of badges and brochures.'[27]

This latter tendency seems to have been widespread, for the district
leader of Frankfurt am Main reported in the same month that PO leaders
were 'no longer seen as Betreuer of the people' and that there were an
increasing number of cases in which 'people did not open the door to
political leaders for fear of having to buy something off them.'[28]

Finally, the position of the party at the outbreak of war was
summed up in a report from the district leader in Wiesbaden in November
1939 in which he emphasized how dependent it was on the prestige of
Hitler who

'through his person forms the main link between
the party and the people. One has to recognize
that we have a long way to go before the party as
such is firmly rooted in the people.'[29]

(e) The party and the war.

The outbreak of war presented the PO with both opportunities
and a big challenge. At the top, Bormann found increasingly favourable
conditions for his attempt to turn the St.d.F.'s office into the
political 'general staff' of the Third Reich, asserting its authority
over both party and state.[30] For the fact that Hitler now devoted
almost all his time to strategic and military questions and was based at
headquarters well away from the government ministries in Berlin enabled
Bormann, who never left his side, gradually to control the
communications between Hitler and most of the government and party
leadership. With the flight of Hess to Scotland in May 1941, Bormann at
last secured official as well as effective control over the St.d.F.'s
office, now renamed the Party Chancellery, and after his official
appointment as the Führer's Secretary in April 1943, he acquired the
formal authority to intervene at will in the whole range of state
responsibilities.

Nevertheless, despite this substantial increase in power,
Bormann and the Party Chancellery still failed to achieve dominance over

either the state or the party. Within the state domain, individual ministers, such as Goebbels with his Propaganda Ministry and, until 1944, Speer with his Armaments Ministry, were too well-entrenched and retained too close links with the Führer to succumb to the Party Chancellery. Above all, however, Himmler and his SS emerged as the main rival of the PO, straddling party and state. With its rapidly expanding military wing, the Waffen SS, with its concentration camp network which was increasingly being utilized as a gigantic labour force for its own independent industrial empire, and with its control over the whole security apparatus of the Reich, to which in 1943 was added the Reich Ministry of the Interior, the SS represented a formidable competitor. For some time Bormann sought to work with Himmler in an alliance against the state apparatus, an association in which Himmler had also advantages, but the political power vacuum which had opened up in the occupied territories lured both party and SS and led inevitably to a growing conflict which was bound to intensify and embrace the Reich itself. Up to the end of the war it remained indecisive. Neither side could subordinate the other because Hitler clearly would not permit it.

To some extent, the formidable appearance of the SS disguised a much less impressive reality. Indeed, in a sense the SS represented a microcosm of the Nazi regime itself - a conglomerate of organizations which operated to a large extent on their own initiative with comparatively little effective coordination. Nevertheless, the SS was not bedevilled by the strong regional basis of the PO. For, although the Party Chancellery expanded its power at the expense of the other Reichsleiter and its authority over the affiliates, the Gauleiter continued to retain much of their independence. Indeed, the war led to a marked increase in the authority of the Gauleiter since, after their appointment as so-called Reich Defence Commissioners, they acquired a growing number of responsibilities for the war effort, particularly in coping with the effects of the allied bombing campaign. Moreover, as the war situation deteriorated, Hitler was inclined to transfer more and more responsibilities to them because of his mistrust of the state bureaucracy. In any case, the growing strain on the whole administration made it more difficult to exercise control from the centre, while the Gauleiter possessed the degree of ruthlessness, contempt for red tape and political weight to take charge and deal with the emergencies on the spot.

Generally, Bormann had welcomed this growth in the authority of the Gauleiter. He had already cooperated with the Interior Ministry in using the opportunity provided by the incorporation of Austria and parts of Poland as integral parts of the Reich, to devise a new form of Gau for these areas - the so-called Reichsgau. These new Reichsgaue united both party and state powers to a far greater extent than in the old Reich, where vested interests had blocked change, forming strong regional centres of authority under the Gauleiter. This reform had been supported by the Interior Ministry under Wilhelm Frick and also by the St.d.F. for similar reasons, namely to counteract the disintegration of· the field administrations of both state and party into numerous more or less autonomous agencies. However, while the Interior Ministry intended the Gauleiter to act as the key regional representatives of the state administration subordinate to the Ministry, Bormann aimed to use them to establish party control over the regional state authorities as subordinates of the St.d.F. These new Reichsgaue were seen as the model for the re-structuring of the rest of Germany after the war; in the meantime, Bormann worked to strengthen the Gauleiter vis-à-vis both state and other party agencies. The assumption behind this policy - the willingness of the Gauleiter to act as regional agents of the St.d.F. - was never realised. Their continuing autonomy, explicitly sanctioned by Hitler, remained a permanent obstacle to Bormann's attempt to turn the PO into an effective field administration for the St.d.F./Party Chancellery. Furthermore, their growing power merely encouraged the progressive disintegration of the whole state administration. This was exacerbated by a parallel tendency for the district leaders also to acquire new responsibilities from the state agencies and, in many cases, to seek to emulate the Gauleiter by establishing their own private domains. In the latter phase of the war this determination of the party cadres to further their own interests and, as a means to this, the particular interests of their areas, seriously complicated the task of those, such as the Armaments Minister, who were responsible for mobilizing the economic resources of the nation in the most effective way.

As Stephen Salter points out in a subsequent essay, this obstructive behaviour by the Gauleiter was partly connected with the fact that, with the outbreak of war, the party was faced with the supreme test in its role of Menschenführung: 'the maintenance and improvement of the nation's morale'.[31] To begin with, the party had few problems in this respect - although the contribution by individual Gauleiter to the successful resistance to the wage cuts attempted by the government on the outbreak of war shows how seriously it took its responsibilities. The succession of German victories proved a highly effective morale-booster, although the negative side of this was a demoralising growth in the prestige of the Army in the eyes of the public. The real test for the party cadre, however, came with the critical phase in the war which began with the defeat at Stalingrad in January 1943.

To overcome the crisis of morale which followed Stalingrad, the PO was urged to redouble its efforts at Betreuung. In particular, the relatives of those killed in the war were to be 'warmly cared for'.[32] It was the duty of the branch leader to break the bad news, offer comfort and advice, invite widows to cultural events, and provide the children with presents for Christmas and birthdays. Above all, however, Bormann set about trying to revive the atmosphere of the pre-1933 period, informing the PO that the 'virtues which characterized the National Socialists in the time of struggle must more than ever be not only preached but also lived.'[33] In the autumn of 1943, he ordered a series of membership meetings at which attendance was compulsory, insisted that members should intensify propaganda by word of mouth, and even demanded that 'every three months the whole party membership of each local branch must march as in earlier times.'[34] There was also a return to the social revolutionary ideas of the pre-1933 period with Bormann encouraging the Gau economic advisers to intervene more and more in business and stressing its accountability to the community in the shape of the party. This mood found expression above all in the confrontation between the party cadre and Speer's armaments administration, dominated as it was by the representatives of large private industry.

The culmination of this attempt to mobilize the party by recreating the atmosphere of the 'time of struggle' and thereby to strengthen the population's will to resist occurred with the formation of the Volkssturm in the autumn of 1944. This attempt at a levée en masse was from the start very much a party affair, for it was financed by the party, organized on a Gau basis and led by the Gauleiter. Badly equipped, incompetently led, bedevilled by jurisdictional conflicts with the SS, a collection of old men and frightened boys kept in line by the fear of summary execution, the Volkssturm was an appropriate finale to the party's attempts at Menschenführung.

Germany's participation in the Second World War did not end in revolution as it had in the First. To this extent, it might be argued that the Nazi Party had succeeded in its main task of sustaining national morale. The evidence, however, does not support such a supposition. Whatever it was that kept the Germans fighting – belief in Hitler, fear of the Gestapo, reasonable food supplies compared with World War I, fear of the Russians, a basic patriotism – the activities of the party, and particularly of the PO, had if anything a negative effect. The political cadre had become fat and complacent, corruption was rife, and the local party leadership had for too long been accustomed to exercising a petty tyranny. Furthermore, the major burden of Betreuung duties carried out by the party fell not on the party cadre but on affiliates such as the NSV. Even here there is evidence that many people preferred the state and municipal services to those provided by the party which were linked to ideological pressures. As far as the mass of the population was concerned, they were prepared to put up with the party so long as Hitler continued to produce spectacular economic and diplomatic achievements. However, the moment the regime began to go sour, it was the local party leadership which bore the brunt of popular resentment. From 1943 onwards, the contrast between poor attendance at party meetings and rising congregations in the churches became a regular refrain in reports by the party cadre and the SD.[35] Under the stress of death, destruction and impending defeat with the gloomy prospects it opened up, people increasingly turned from the bogus, ersatz pastoral care of the party to their traditional source of spiritual consolation – the Churches. It was a measure of the party's failure to fulfill the task set for it by Hitler in 1933 of moulding the German into a 'new man'.[36]

Notes

1. Wahl to Hitler 25 June 1941 quoted in D. Orlow, The History of the Nazi Party 1933–1945 (Newton Abbot, 1973), vol.2 p.341.

2. Röver (?) Denkschrift 1942, Bundesarchiv Koblenz (BA) NS 20/109.

3. The term PO to describe the political organization of the party was officially banned by Hess in 1935 on the grounds that it suggested that the political organization was a distinct formation of the party, whereas 'the NSDAP is in its totality a political organization...which embraces all party comrades'. Der Stellvertreter des Führers Anordnung Nr. 157/35 27.7.1935 BA NS 6/220. Despite the ban, the term PO is a useful one which will, therefore, be employed in this paper to describe the political cadre of the Nazi party.

4.   Loeper to the Reichsleitung 28.11.1929 BA Slg. Schumacher 204.

5.   Kube to the Reichsleitung 29.12.1930 BA Slg. Schumacher 205.

6.   Hitler Denkschrift 20.12.1932 BA NS 22/356.

7.   Parteistatistik 1 Januar 1935. Hrsg. der Reichsorganisationsleiter der NSDAP. (München, 1935), Bd. 2 pp.284-5.

8.   Hans Witt to Adolf Hitler 19.7.1933 Berlin Document Centre, Personalakte Erich Koch.

9.   BA R 43 II/995.

10.   Heeresadjutant bei Hitler 1938-1943. Aufzeichnungen des Majors Engel. Hrsg. Hildegard von Kotze. Schriftenreihe der Vierteljahrshefte für Zeitgeschichte Nr. 29 (Stuttgart, 1974), pp.37,39.

11.   Hans Mommsen, Beamtentum im Dritten Reich (Stuttgart, 1966), pp.35-6.

12.   Hitler Denkschrift 20.12.1933 BA NS 22/356.

13.   NSDAP. Der Führer. Verfügung 45/44 28.2.1944 BA R 43 II/1194b.

14.   Bormann Vermerk 20.2.1939 BA Slg. Schumacher 371.

15.   Peter Diehl-Thiele, Partei und Staat im Dritten Reich. Untersuchungen zum Verhältnis von NSDAP und allgemeiner innerer Staatsverwaltung. Münchener Studien zur Politik Bd. 9 (München, 1969), pp.164-165.

16.   Ibid. pp.167-168.

17.   For the following membership figures see Aryeh L. Unger, The Totalitarian Party and People in Nazi Germany and Soviet Russia (Cambridge, 1974), pp.83-85.

18.   Parteistatistik 1 January 1935. op.cit. Bd.1 pp.155,162.

19.   Der Stellvertreter des Führers. Anordnung 30.5.1934 BA NS 6/16.

20.   NSDAP Kreisleitung Hildesheim-Land an die Gauleitung Hannover-Süd-Braunschweig 13.1.1934 Tätigkeitsbericht für den Monat Dezember 1933 BA NS 22/618.

21.   See Bormann to Ley 24.4.1936 BA NS 22/713.

22.   For the following see Reichsministerium der Finanzen. Vermerk über den Reichszuschuss für die Partei und ihre Gliederungen 14.12.1942 BA R 2/31096.

23.   Denkschrift Florians betr. Nachwuchsbildung des Politischen Leiter-Korps im Gau Düsseldorf. Copy enclosed in Stellvertreter des Führers Rundschreiben 72/39 4.4.1939 BA NS 6/232.

24. Kreis Oberwesterwald Monat Juli 1939 betr. Mitgliederappelle in den Ortsgruppen Hauptstaatsarchiv Wiesbaden (HSAW) 483/5543.

25. Partei-Kanzlei. Bericht vom Gau München-Oberbayern 18.12.44 BA NS 6/291.

26. Erich Kordt, Wahn und Wirklichkeit (Stuttgart, 1947), pp.44f.

27. Kreisleitung der NSDAP Rheingau-St.Goarshausen. Politischer Lagebericht Mai/Juni 1939 HSAW 483/5536.

28. Kreisleitung Gross-Frankfurt a/M Politischer Lagebericht Juni/Juli 1939 HSAW 483/5543.

29. Kreisleitung Wiesbaden. Stimmungsbericht November 1939 HSAW 483/5550.

30. Bormann Vermerk 11.5.1943 BA Slg. Schumacher 371.

31. Arbeitspläne der Reichsleitung der NSDAP für den Einsatz der Partei und der angeschlossener Verbände im A-Falle. Hrsg. von der Abteilung M des Stabs des Stellvertreters des Führers 16.5.1938. Aufgaben im Kriegsfalle. BA NS 6/379.

32. Parteikanzlei Rundschreiben Nr. 2/43 7.1.43 BA NS 6/340.

33. Parteikanzlei Rundschreiben Nr. 37/43 1.3.43 BA NS 6/167.

34. Parteikanzlei Anordnung A 56/43 30.9.1943 BA NS 6/167.

35. See, for example, the excerts from the Weltanschauliche Berichte der Kreisschulungsämter 1943-1944 in Bayern in der NS-Zeit. Soziale Lage und politisches Verhalten der Bevölkerung im Spiegel vertraulicher Berichte. Hrsg. von Martin Broszat, Elke Fröhlich, Falk Wiesemann (München, Wien, 1977), pp.571ff.

36. Hitler told a gathering of SA and SS leaders in Bad Reichenhall on 1 July 1933 that 'the essence of the revolution had not exhausted itself in the take-over of power' but that they had to 'create a new man'. BA R 43 II/995.

2. Recreating the Civil Service : Issues and Ideas in the Nazi Regime

JANE CAPLAN

1. The Problem of Party-State Relations

> 'It is correct and to the point to say that the civil servant is no longer a servant of the state, but a servant of the community (Volksgemeinschaft). However, the latter is represented by the Party...False is the formulation: the civil servant is the totality of the servants of the people (die Gesamtheit der Diener des Volkes). This is another intrusion of superseded formal political thought. Maybe that used to be the case. But not today. There are many servants of the people in the above sense who are in the Party and the armed forces. In this sense it might be truer to say that the servants of the people are all those who have sworn their loyalty to the Führer.'[1]

The victim of this painstaking critique was one of the candidates for the higher civil service qualifying examination in 1936, who had answered a question on the relationship between civil service and state. His examiner's comments were forwarded up to the president of the examination commission, on the grounds that the young man's writing contained a series of worrying discrepancies with what was described as 'the standard Party opinion'; but we should also be alert to the examiner's own difficulty in expressing precisely what was the right line, and perhaps even to a hint of regret in his reference to what had once been the case in the past. For if the unfortunate examinee was confused, so also were many of his elders. The issue of party-state relations, with its practical implications for the status of the civil service, was not just unsettled and controversial, but politically explosive. Academic and professional careers were being made and broken on it; and while political leaders made rhetorical and conflicting declarations which confused the actual, the practicable, and the ideal, civil servants themselves struggled to find practical interpretations which would satisfy the demands of administrative efficiency without giving political offence in too many quarters at once.

The conceptual confusion, amply documented in the academic literature and in the boiled-down versions reproduced in the professional press,[2] mirrored a disorderly reality whose dimensions, and ultimately devastating effects, gradually became inescapably evident. The unanimity with which an administrative crisis, or set of crises, was acknowledged in both party and state quarters by the early years of the war is impressive. By then, the diagnoses and cures being proposed were very various, as also were the moods and tones of the commentators, which ranged from truculence to despair. However, common to almost all of them was the sense that Germany's administrative apparatus was out of control: too large, too fragmented, too unwieldy; its motivations and principles discordant instead of politically harmonious; not only incapable of mastering its tasks, but actually creating new problems for itself: a bureaucratic leviathan.

Historians seeking to describe and explain the processes that led to the regime's surprisingly self-conscious verdicts on its own failings face a particular difficulty in the very variety and ubiquity of the evidence of crisis. There is virtually never a time between 1933 and 1945 when major governmental figures are not entangled in internecine conflicts and complaining vigorously that each other's conduct is making efficient administration impossible. Explanation of this cannot easily resort to a simple chronological model of decline from stability to chaos, even if this image tends to be encouraged by the documentary evidence, since those responsible for it wanted to represent their recent history as an unfortuante descent from the honourable aspirations of 1933 to the abject deficiencies of ten years on. The structural ubiquity of complaint is also difficult to handle historically; it means that there are no fully representative judgments (except in terms of cumulation), but only numerous variant voices, speaking more often to internal audiences than directly to the objects of their criticism, and also frequently found in shifting and unpredictable alliances. It is not surprising, to take an example, to find an outburst from the interior minister Frick against Hess's belated rejection of a civil servant's appointment after the documents had been processed and signed by Frick himself,

> 'It's quite impossible to run an appointments policy like this. From today onwards I refuse to send an appointment proposal with my signature to [Hess] only to have him then reject it...'[3]

Political lines of a familiar 'Party/state' division seem clearly enough drawn here, but what is to be made of the cross-currents in a case like the following? In August 1941 Bormann (now head of the NSDAP Party Chancellery) writes to the head of the Reich Chancellery, Lammers, to pass on complaints from Gauleiters that they are being bombarded by central Reich offices with communications about the state of disputes among themselves.

> 'The Gauleiters point out with some justification that it really does not contribute to the strengthening of the authority of Reich agencies if individual offices choose to bring their differences of opinion with other offices to the notice of the Gauleiters and other subordinates...'

Within the comparatively short time of a month, the two chancelleries agree to issue separate but co-ordinated instructions to the Party and the state respectively: Lammers's order invokes the Führer as having forbidden the communication of disputes etc. to subordinate agencies because this contravenes National Socialist discipline and implies that the state lacks 'clarity of purpose'. Six months later we find a dispute of exactly this kind being referred to Lammers - a row between the interior and finance ministries over the former's handling of a change in the system of housing subsidies for civil servants.[4] The currents running through this cannot be assigned to a simple dualism, but reveal (as many other examples could) complex combinations of interest and division.

The hubbub backstage is all the more striking if it is contrasted with the smooth image of control, convergence and community that formed the propaganda image of the 'Third Reich'. Volksgemeinschaft and Gleichschaltung (community and co-ordination) were obviously supposed to convey the reality of Hitler's Germany to its own population, and doubtless were actually the conscious (if futile) aim and hope of many who identified themselves with the politics of National Socialism. Certainly, an earlier generation of critical observers of Nazi Germany was not unwilling to accept this image. Thus Otto Kirchheimer, a distinguished exile from Nazism, wrote in 1941:

> 'In short, the idea of technical rationality
> which underlies the new governmental organization
> actually finds its nearest approximation in a
> perfectly running, though complicated, piece of
> machinery...[It is] aimed only at the certainty
> that every order will produce an exactly
> calculable reaction.'[5]

Some years later, the Nuremberg prosecutors, faced with overwhelming documentary evidence of the Nazi regime's fragmentation, took refuge in the belief that the seething reality was kept in control by the ruthless determination of a few key personalities - a view which is echoed by more recent historians who regard the regime's shapelessness and unpredictability as the deliberate creation of Hitler. Currently, other historians are seeking to demonstrate that on the contrary this shapelessness was no-one's deliberate creation, and that its effects at the level of policy-making and execution were complex, displaced, and often negative. In summary, they contend that the Nazi regime never developed a unity or stability of its own, but remained 'parasitic' on existing political and social institutions, including the state machinery itself. Never able to generate the conditions for its own stabilisation, the regime thus progressively perverted or decomposed the institutions it had inherited, thereby consuming the basis of its own existence. The cause according to this view, was the pre-1933 character of the NSDAP itself, as essentially a force directed towards the political mobilisation of the elements it needed to bring it into power. Propaganda, and not programme , was the Party's ideological vehicle, and its sole objective (in terms of planning) was the seizure of power, not its exercise. This concentrated but restricted sense of purpose was paralleled by an internal organizational structure which was designed to ensure Hitler's sole authority as Führer. As a consequence, the party lacked any institutional means for the handling or solving of conflicts - a negative attribute which was in effect transferred to the political system as a whole after 1933. Movement and regime were thus structurally founded upon contradiction, and condemned to the consequences of this.[6]

The civil service was, of course, one of the most important
of the institutions 'inherited' by the Nazi regime, one which was both
the subject and object of these processes of decomposition. This essay
will aim to summarise the principal approaches to civil service policy
within the regime and to explain the differences between them. However,
it is necessary to begin with a brief look at the themes of
administrative and civil service politics before 1933: not only to
provide the usual sense of context, but in particular to show how the
Nazi regime was also the heir to problems not of its own making - even
though its distinctive contribution was in the end to aggravate rather
than resolve them.

2. The Background - the Civil Service in the Weimar Republic.

Quo Vadis Deutsches Berufsbeamtentum [+] demanded the title
of an NSDAP propaganda pamphlet of 1932, giving equal prominence to
that hackneyed motto of Frederick the Great, 'Ich bin der erster Diener
meines Staates'.[*] The anonymous author (doubtless a member of the
NSDAP's recently established civil service department) began by
repudiating the electoral tactic of bribing the voter with promises:
'The NSDAP promises nothing', he wrote, in a flourish characteristic of
his party's general claim to have broken with the politics of party
self-interest, but he continued with the assertion that 'the party
stands firm on the platform of the Berufsbeamtentum, and...it would
create this civil service if it were not already in existence'. Where
was this institution going in 1932? It was a serious question, and was
being asked across the political spectrum at this time, partly because
of the structural problem of the relationship between civil service and
state stability, partly because of the importance of public sector
employment in economic policy. For a German audience the term
Berufsbeamtentum would have had multiple connotations which are not
adequately conveyed by the translation 'professional civil service'.
The most prominent meaning would probably have been the conception of
the civil service as a privileged social and political institution - a
theme as dominant in German (and especially Prussian) history as
parliament was for English history. At its most rarified, the civil
service could be seen not just as the delegates of the state, the
executive of its authority, but as the embodiment of the very essence of
sovereign power. The classic moments in the formation of this
institution (corresponding, to use the parliamentary analogy, to moments
like Magna Carta, 1688 and so on) would be seen as the Prussia of
Frederick the Great and later of the Reform Era, and the Germany of the
Kaisers. The debatable relationship between concept and historical
reality can't detain us here, though we must at least note that it was
not unproblematic, even before the revolution of 1919.[7] However, it
was the revolution that, as the foremost commentator on civil service
matters wrote in 1928, made the civil service into 'a genuine
problem'.[8]

Synthetic or not, the image of civil service homogeneity and

+ Where are you going German professional civil service?
* 'I am the first servant of my state.'

political centrality was shaken both by the postwar social upheaval, and by the establishment of a parliamentary state with cabinet responsibility in place of the authoritarian constitutional monarchy served by an executive government. Of course, political opinion after 1918 diverged sharply on the magnitude of the convulsion, on whether it had been desirable or deplorable, and whether the changes and tendencies it had provoked should be pursued further, reversed, or perhaps deflected into some entirely different course.

There was, therefore, a good deal of political capital to be made out of the state of the civil service in the Weimar Republic; it could be used as a stick with which to beat a particular party (most often the SPD) or the Republic itself, and also as a source of mass electoral support, numbering as it did around a million voters. As well as this, there was a clear connexion between civil service matters on the one hand, and constitutional and administrative policies on the other. Throughout the life of the Republic, the problem of 'the improvised democracy'[9] was closely associated with the possibility that its instabilities might be resolved by restoring political authority to the executive. This debate had become a clamour after 1930, when the economic crisis threw the issue of governmental competence and constitutional stability into further prominence. To say that there was a clear movement towards a more authoritarian resolution of these issues after 1930 is not to attribute inevitability to the process, far less to the further twist of Hitler's appointment as chancellor in January 1933. However, there was during this time much cultivation in government and academic circles of the idea that the existing state was incapable of generating effective responses to the tremendous social problems provoked by economic collapse. By the early 1930s, the battle for power at the top was being fought out among only those most committed to radical political reform: Brüning, Papen, Schleicher, Hitler. These were certainly representatives of very different constellations of social and political power, but were linked by their despair at or antipathy to the institution of parliamentary democracy.

At one level, then, the civil service elite was the obvious candidate for the political authority that the parliamentary system seemed unable to guarantee. At the same time, however, as Papen's Preussenstreich[*] of July 1932 demonstrated, a relocation of political power was closely connected with the reform of German federalism: a constitutional and an administrative issue, turning on the question of whether a less parliamentary Germany would also be a more unitary Germany. Furthermore, the 'administration' was not simply the ministerial civil servants who were beginning to overshadow parliament and cabinet, nor simply the apparatuses of the state: it was also a huge peopled institution whose scale and legal rights (to pay, tenure, and pensions) were a drain on the budget and a further fiscal strain on federalism (in the sense of disturbing the financial relations between the central state, the Länder, and local authorities). Already in the mid-1920s crisis of stabilization, severe reductions in the size of the civil service had been enforced, and these remained as a recent experience which the NSDAP was not slow to exploit in its propaganda. Even more recently, the relatively generous 1927 salary scales had been

* take-over of the Prussian state government

cut by up to 23% under Brüning's emergency orders – an action which, it
has been argued, strained civil servants' loyalties to breaking point
and further undermined the sense of the state's stability.[10]   The
coexistence of these different currents muddied the waters of both
propaganda and policy before 1933, and ensured that the strategic
options available to the Nazi regime would be highly contradictory.

3. The Civil Service in the Third Reich – Programmes and
    Personalities.

        One obvious way of defining the fundamental differences
within the Nazi regime in the field of civil service politics is to
distinguish between a basically favourable and a basically antagonistic
attitude to the civil service. Thus Martin Broszat has described

> 'two opposing tendencies...; the one...derived
> from a basically positive evaluation of the civil
> service and sought to take up the tendency
> towards the authoritarian executive state
> (Beamtenstaat) which was already under
> construction in the period of presidential rule;
> it sought to develop this further in combination
> with the National Socialist Führerprinzip, in the
> direction of an elitist leadership role for the
> civil service'.

He suggests that the strongest proponent of this view was the interior
minister Wilhelm Frick, but that it was also found among those younger
members of the civil service who sympathised with Nazism and in the
NSDAP's own civil service organization, the Hauptamt für Beamte and
Reichsbund der Deutschen Beamten, led by Hermann Neef. Broszat's second
tendency 'derived from a basic mistrust of the civil service', and was
found among the NSDAP's old guard (alte Kämpfer) and the party's
functionaries. These took the view that a truly National Socialist
state could never incorporate or rest upon the traditional civil
service, because (consistent with its history as a political
institution) it would always remain a state within the state.[11]

        The two tendencies were clearly opposing, yet Broszat also
argues that they were not necessarily entirely incompatible; the fact
that they proved to be so in practice was due to the fundamental fiction
of National Socialism: that it was built ideologically and politically
on a unitary and cohesive state. Because this was a fiction, it was
impossible for agreement to be reached on the actual shape and function
of the new, politicised civil service, appropriate to the new state,
which in principle was wanted. Moreover we could add to this the point
that the process of maintaining the illusion itself contributed further
confusion and aroused other antagonisms, as the opening section of this
essay suggested. Broszat's model offers a useful starting-point,
especially in sketching out a fluid series of sub-groups, and not simply
a rigid dualism. By looking in more detail at these groups, we will be
able to understand Broszat's own conclusion, that in Nazi Germany a
refoundation of the civil service was both necessary, and impossible.

(a) Wilhelm Frick

The first 'group' is in fact an individual, Wilhelm Frick, but his institutional position as head of a ministry may justify including him as an independent tendency. Frick was one of the two other National Socialists who joined the coalition cabinet formed by Hitler in January 1933. His appointment as interior minister gave the Nazis the most sensitive point in the system of public security, after the presidency and chancellorship. Although the Reich interior ministry had no field machinery of its own (internal affairs being the prerogative of the Länder), it was the co-ordinating centre for constitutional, administrative, and civil service affairs, for police matters, and for public health, welfare and education. Its political significance had already been enhanced by the preceding years of decree rule and constitutional shrinkage; and although the NSDAP leadership as such had not devoted much attention to the details of a constitutional reform, Frick himself had a strong and stubborn sense that he was called upon to do great things for Germany and National Socialism – in effect, to give Germany a new state. By most accounts, Frick was an austere, self-important and in the end weak man. Born in 1877, he had trained as a senior civil servant in the administration; at the end of the war, he had been appointed to the political department of the Munich police, but was transferred to the criminal side after refusing allegiance to the new state. His connexions with Hitler date from this period, and his own complicity in the 1923 putsch earned him a suspended prison sentence of 15 months. Turning to a more open form of political activity, he was elected to the Reichstag in 1924 on a völkisch ticket, and subsequently became the leader of the NSDAP fraction – a public position which gave him the reputation of being one of Hitler's closest associates and spokesmen.

In the 1920s, Frick was a frequent speaker on civil service issues in the Reichstag, the typical mode of Nazi intervention being (as in most questions) the combination of scabrous attack and declaratory demand. In a typical speech in July 1925, criticising the forced reduction of civil service personnel, he stated that

> 'There are two categories of civil servants with whom we do think it is right and proper for staff reductions to begin. The first are the so-called 'Revolutionsbeamte'. The situation is at its most flagrant in Severing's state [Prussia]. These creatures [i.e. Marxist trade union and party functionaries] are none of them trained for a civil service career. The other category are members of the Jewish race. We regard it as beneath our dignity to allow ourselves to be governed by people of this race.'[12]

Frick returned again and again to these themes, which formed the typical content of the NSDAP's civil service propaganda in the 1920s, together with the demand for the adjustment of salaries in favour of the lowest-paid. In December 1928, Frick could have been heard making the following declarations, rich with ambiguity for the future: alleging that the most senior civil servants were paid far too much, he claimed that

'The social democrats have a particular interest
in giving preferential treatment to ministerial
civil servants, because with this they hope to
procure themselves willing helpers in their
takeover of the state machinery. Many a civil
servant forgets that there is no greater and more
dangerous enemy for the professional civil
service than the social democrats and their
minister Severing [at this time interior minister
in Müller's cabinet]. The professional civil
service is being systematically destroyed by
them: on the one hand from above, in that it is
being more and more undermined and corrupted by
party politics; and on the other from below, as,
on the basis of the Personalabbauverordnung [the
law enforcing staff reductions], of the law on
railway officials and the salary law, the
professional civil service is being dismantled,
and civil servants demoted to the status of
wage-earners and clerks.'[13]

    In January 1930, Frick was appointed joint education and
interior minister in the right-wing coalition cabinet in Thuringia, a
post he held until the break-up of the coalition in April 1931.
Evidently his brief from Hitler was to rehearse on behalf of the NSDAP
the kind of administrative (and educational) policies the party would be
aiming at nationally when the time came, and to undertake 'a slow
purification of the administrative and civil service apparatus from the
red revolutionists'.[14] Not surprisingly, Frick began with the police,
defending his purge as a policy of appointing 'trained civil servants,
qualified for their profession'.[15]

    By this time Frick, once known as 'the royal Bavarian Nazi',
had apparently managed to impress Hitler as a fanatical National
Socialist, a tough and disciplined professional; but according to
another view (that of Otto Strasser) at the same time he was 'a typical
average civil servant...definitely not leadership material...a nice
fellow and a decent enough chap.'[16] Overall, we should not be
satisfied to judge Frick solely in terms of his views on the structure
of the administration, for he was also a convinced antisemite and
committed to the regime's racialist policies. Nevertheless, in our more
limited field he does stand out as an ultra-nationalist and
authoritarian, rather than a rabid populist - perhaps in fact the very
type of extreme conservative who found the NSDAP more congenial than the
DNVP because of its fanatical antisemitism. His conservatism on the
question of the state comes out clearly in his public statements as well
as through his ministerial policy; in a 1934 article, for instance, he
argued that 'state' was 'a generic term' which comprehended both Party
and Volk - an extremely heretical statement of a kind for which lesser
figures had suffered.[17] Frick's sponsorship of such views from his
position as interior minister had an ambiguous significance. On the one
hand, it preserved a degree of continuity with conservative concepts of
the state and bureaucracy and doubtless made the ministry to some extent
a haven for those who shared these views. On the other hand, his
stubborn insistence on a traditionalist concept of his ministry, of its
administrators and their norms also ensured the progressive

marginalization of both the ministry and the bundle of attitudes
associated with it, as Frick's ambitions outreached his actual power.

The vision that animated Frick throughout his tenure of the
ministry (he was kicked upstairs in 1943, and replaced by Himmler) was
of a comprehensive reform of Germany's constitutional and administrative
structure - a project premised on precisely that political uniformity
that the NSDAP promised but never realised. The fact that Frick's
schemes were frustrated was not simply due to the inherent
'irrationalism' of the Nazi state, except to the extent that this was
itself the outcome of the stalemating of political conflict in that
system.[18] For Frick's massive schemes were in themselves no more
'rational' than the other current versions of national unity with which
they competed: all were premised on illusions of unity, whether of the
NSDAP as the form of the unity of the Volk, or the professional civil
service as the form of unity of the state. Just as the NSDAP's
political visions were thorough-going misrepresentations of the origins
and meaning of political conflict in the republic, and hence could not
be any kind of resolution, so also Frick's grand unitary design
misconstrued the equally problematic issue of constitutional reform.
His conception of a politically centralised, administratively
decentralised unitary state, pivoted internally on the interior
ministry, implied a pre-eminent role for an elite of civil servants.
They would be the active bearers of the new state: National Socialism
would be their inspiring ideology rather than being an independent or
competing element in the power structure. However, even on an optimum
assessment of the chances for realising such an executive system, it
would have required the active co-operation of those other ministries
with direct responsibilities in the administrative field, principally
the finance and justice ministries, and the Reich chancellery. Yet
Frick's ambitions neither convinced nor disarmed his potential allies,
whose suspicions led them to form only a series of shifting tactical
alliances rather than constructing a firm front. Perhaps Frick's old
association with the Nazi party also made him suspect to ministers like
Krosigk, Gürtner and Lammers, who evidently put a certain premium on
maintaining their own distance from the Party itself. Frick thus became
increasingly isolated from both his Party comrades and his ministerial
and bureaucratic colleagues. Hitler eventually numbered him among those
Nazis who had once done wonders for the movement, but had since proved
unable to adapt to the demands of National Socialist rule - an
unintentional irony, no doubt.

A number of Frick's senior associates in the interior
ministry could well be put alongside him, on the basis of belonging to
the same generation, though none had the same length or depth of
association with the NSDAP. Perhaps the closest in both respects was
Hans Fabricius, some years younger than Frick (he was born in 1891), and
in general something of a junior version of his minister. He had made
his civil service career in the financial administration, until his
political activities led to his suspension in November 1929 and his
dismissal, after disciplinary proceedings, in March 1930.[19] He joined
the NSDAP in September 1929, got a Reichstag seat a year later, and was
secretary of the NSDAP fraction. He returned to the civil service in
1933, to a post in the interior ministry's newly reorganized civil
service section; he also held the senior honorary position in the Nazi
civil service organization in Berlin, and was a prominent propagandist

and prolific writer in these circles. Typifying the image of the civil
service he wanted to promote was the title of a 1934 article
'Schöpferisches Beamtentum' - 'Creative Civil Service'; or his short
book Der Beamte einst und im neuen Reich (1933), with its chapter on
'The professional civil service - bearer of the state', and its studied
neglect of the party.

(b) Hans Pfundtner

Nearer to Frick in age, though less close in political
experience, was the principal state secretary in the interior ministry
Hans Pfundtner, born in 1881. He had had an orthodox civil service
career until 1919, when he left the civil service after refusing to take
the new oath of loyalty, and took up a commercial career. In March 1932
he left the DNVP and the next day applied to join the NSDAP (this was
two days after Goebbels had addressed the prestigious National Club, of
which Pfundtner was a member). In the months that followed, Pfundtner
pestered various Party leaders with policy projects and draft articles,
stressing the potential value of his network of contacts, asking the
Party to emphasise its commitment to the civil service, and even
proposing himself as an electoral candidate in July 1932, on the grounds
that he could be 'link-man to the ministerial civil service'. Appointed
as Frick's state secretary on 2 February 1933, Pfundtner showed a
perfect readiness to participate in the regime's purge of the civil
service and violation of its rights, and he lent himself to the public
defence of this 'restoration of a professional civil service'. In
selling himself so avidly to the regime, however, Pfundtner was also
selling out the mass civil service, and thus undermining his own chosen
platform. By the early 1940s, years of neglect of civil servants'
rights had also been years of conflict and defeat for their self-elected
champions, and Pfundtner eventually became deeply involved in schemes to
restore to the service the status and prestige that his own earlier
activities had helped vitiate.

The ultimate crisis of the civil service was no doubt felt
most deeply by this group of men who had hoped to align their politics
and their professionalism in large-scale reforms. The second of the
groups to be discussed, the younger generation of Nazi sympathisers, had
invested similar aspirations in a civil service-based revivification of
the German polity, but their responses to disappointment were more
complex, since their age made it more difficult for them to withdraw or
resign. I have chosen here to look at two men who, in different ways,
signalled a profound dissent with the regime they had once
enthusiastically supported.

(c) Wilhelm Stuckart

Wilhelm Stuckart, second state secretary in the interior
ministry, was born in 1902, the son of a railway worker in Wiesbaden.
After university he worked in a bank before taking his first civil
service examination, a fact that suggests that he may have had to
support himself while preparing for a civil service career. He
qualified in 1930, but spent no more than two years in the
administration, resigning under political pressure in 1932. He had

already been active in the ultra-right as a student, and had first
joined the NSDAP as early as 1922. After the refoundation of the Party,
he had acted as a legal adviser but did not formally rejoin until 1930.
This long association with the NSDAP reflects the depth of Stuckart's
political commitment, and he was given high office in the new regime in
June 1933, when he was taken into the education ministry as state
secretary. In 1934 he was able to protect himself in a serious quarrel
with his minister by addressing a direct appeal to Hitler himself, who
intervened to prevent Stuckart from being consigned to provincial
oblivion.[20] In March 1935 he took over the interior ministry
department on the constitution and legislation, keeping his courtesy
title of state secretary, and then getting full promotion to the rank in
1938. Stuckart was unusual in his social background (though it is not
entirely clear what level of job his father had), and he undeniably made
his career with and through National Socialism. As state secretary he
held a position of considerable importance, and both his published and
unpublished writings, as well as his day-to-day contributions to
ministerial business, demonstrate that he held very firm opinions on the
subject of administrative organization, opinions which he strove to put
into practice. His personal assistant assessed him after the war as 'a
convinced Nazi' whose convictions had weakened as time went on - a
conventional formula of disillusion and exculpation.[21] He made in
fact a number of unsuccessful attempts from May 1940 to be released from
his job into military service, this being a not uncommon device of the
time to register a concealed loss of political faith.[22]

In practice and in his writings, Stuckart was a strong
defender on pragmatic grounds of the integrity of the state
administration. Despite his postwar protestations that the interior
ministry had progressively lost ground to the Reich chancellery as the
lynchpin in policy-making, it is clear that this was a situation he
deplored and did his best to resist. In the context of this period, his
sense of the characteristics and priorities of an efficient
administrative system was unusually acute, and he was not reticent in
his criticism of the deficiencies he saw around him. From October 1939
he was working with a brief to investigate wide areas of the
administration with a view to simplifying and decentralising it; and
although practical achievements were more or less ruled out, he
developed on paper a comprehenseive scheme for rationalising the entire
administrative structure of 'Greater Germany'. Like Frick, Stuckart's
principal concern was to see the field administration unified, by
restricting the independence of the specialist agencies. His model
(again echoing, and perhaps influencing Frick) was a small, streamlined
interior ministry, which would have supervisory authority over a single
system of field agencies; these could then be delegated with the
exercise of wide local powers. This pattern was not achieved throughout
Germany, but it was prefigured in the administrative structure of the
ten Reichsgaue (seven in the 'Ostmark' (Austria), plus the Sudetenland,
Danzig-Westpreussen, and Wartheland). Although Stuckart also devoted
himself in published and unpublished essays to the recurrent problem of
relations between party and state, he was no more successful than anyone
else in achieving a reconciliation between the ideologically desirable,
and the practically feasible. In his earlier writings, Stuckart took a
more dynamic view of the problem than either Frick or Pfundtner, and -
typical for the contemporary quest for the right formula - proposed that
party and state were effectively combined in the overarching concept of

'Reich'. Yet he seemed to want to avoid committing himself to any final statement about the actual distribution of power. Indeed, he rested his hopes in an effective co-operation between party and state at the highest level, so that the inevitable frictions on the ground could be resolved by reference upwards to the point where the different perspectives converged in a shared political commitment: a futile hope, if we remember that this convergence was precisely what was not achieved.[23]

In later and more private writings, however, Stuckart can be seen struggling with the contradictions created by the impossibility of locating coherent demarcations between the spheres of party and state. A typical observation, from an essay of 1940, reads:

> 'In the National Socialist state therefore, the administration is no longer what it was in the liberal constitutional state [Rechtsstaat] which was paralysed by its own norms. Then it was a technical apparatus for the application of those norms; but now it is the living means of the political leadership for fashioning public life from within the state. In its most comprehensive sense, therefore, administration today basically means nothing other than the preservation of the community and the framing of public life in accordance with the directives of the political leadership.'[24]

The rest of this essay is a detailed discussion of an educational and training system for the civil servants who would run an administration conceived on those lines, a discussion which in fact became the basis for serious policy proposals in the ministry. Stuckart's fears and priorities are clear:

> 'It is now high time to free the higher administrative civil servant from the odium of the lawyer, which he neither is nor should be if he is to understand his calling correctly and correctly perform his job...[The administrative civil servant] must nowadays take part in the preservation and the shaping of the state and the community in his sector. What we need are men who are pioneers of culture, colonisers and political and economic creators in the best sense of these words.[25]

The problem that stands exposed in these enthusiatic acclamations of administrative creativity is, of course, that, far from describing an approach complementary to the NSDAP, it bids precisely to rival the party on its own ground. It is not a solution to the problems of grass-roots conflict that Stuckart had identified, but a description of their morphology.

(d)   Graf von der Schulenburg

A close friend of Stuckart's who shared the discussion of these ideas in their formative stages was Fritz-Dietlof, Graf von der Schulenburg, who, though less prominent in the Nazi period, is now the better remembered as a figure in the 1944 resistance movement. Schulenburg, born in 1902, was a conservative and paternalist patriot, who had hoped to find in Nazism the key to the moral and national regeneration of the German people.[26]   An exuberant nationalist, he joined the NSDAP in 1931, apparently already aware of its demonic side but swayed nevertheless by its dynamic energy.   His devotion to the classic ideals of the Prussian bureaucracy (which he served as a field official in the interior administration) was exaggerated and even fanatic, and his political beliefs were so rigidly elitist that he seems almost to caricature even the extreme paternalism of his class and profession.   However, within the terms of this narrow ethic he was surprisingly outspoken in defence of his beliefs after 1933, exposing himself to risky criticism for his unorthodoxy.   In a 1938 lecture, 'The Prussian Heritage and the National Socialist State', he set out to consider whether Nazism was compatible with his romantic Prussianism. The choice of subject, and its treatment, hinted at Schulenburg's unhappiness with actual political developments, though he tried to square the circle by declaring that since Nazism was a creative force, and the Prussian civil service a creative institution, the two must stand together.   The civil service's task would then be

> 'to cast National Socialism in the metallically hard Prussian mould...to unite National Socialist dynamism with Prussian political experience, [for] National Socialism is the political idea of our age, and Prussianism is the law of our national political life.   And the idea must be forged in accordance with the laws of political life.'[27]

Because of this commitment to a Prussianised bureaucratic elitism as the indispensable foundation for a German renewal, it was the Nazi subversion of this deep conviction that distressed him most.   In 1937 he had already submitted to four ministries a memo entitled 'The Civil Service.   Crisis and Remedy', in which he openly expressed his fears that a creative and responsible and non-bureaucratic civil service was crucial to national welfare, yet that these very values were being dissipated and destroyed under National Socialism.[28]   Like Stuckart, Schulenburg applied to join the armed forces in 1940; and he spent the early war years in and out of the army and various departments of the administration.   He hoped, like others of his class and status, that the regime might be regenerated from within, and addressed some of his reconstruction schemes to Himmler.   He was arrested and executed after the July 1944 plot.

(e)   Reichsbund der Deutschen Beamten

Both of the groups we have looked at so far had the ambiguous advantage of occupying senior positions in the administration – ambiguous in the sense that they rose from these launching-pads of ambition to defeat and frustration. The third and final group of protagonists of the civil service, the NSDAP's own civil service organization, was of a quite different stamp as far as its members' status in the civil service itself was concerned. Membership of the NSDAP's mass civil service association, the Reichsbund der Deutschen Beamten, allegedly covered 98% of all civil servants in 1938; but the officials of the Reichsbund (and its associated party office, the Hauptamt für Beamte) were overwhelmingly middle-grade civil servants, often from the mass employment sectors of the service like the railways and postal system. These represented in fact the authentic voice of the civil service as far as it had made itself heard within National Socialism before 1933. The party's leadership had never cultivated close relations with higher civil servants before the 'seizure of power', in contrast to its well-known contacts with industrialists; and its propaganda and organizational efforts had been largely confined to wooing civil servants en masse, as we have seen above. (It is true that there had also been some attempts to infiltrate party members into key posts, but there is a significant difference between infiltration on the one hand, and the cultivation of existing officials on the other; and this was a distinction that persisted throughout the regime, with the party always giving priority to infiltration.)

(f) Hermann Neef

As an example of this group there is no need to look further than to the head of the Reichsbund and Hauptamt für Beamte, Hermann Neef. Born in 1904, Neef had made his career in the middle grade of the customs service (a sector which had been notorious before 1933 for the number of Nazis allegedly active in it). He joined the NSDAP and the SA in 1923, and was both a local government councillor (Stadtverordneter) and party official in Berlin from 1929 to 1931. There followed a period of obscurity when he had to resign from the council after a family scandal; but his patron in the party, Gauleiter Jakob Sprenger, managed to protect him and preserve his party status. Sprenger had been responsible for the first steps in the organization of civil servants in the NSDAP before 1933, and when he was called to higher office in the regime, it was Neef who stepped into his shoes. Through 1933-4, Neef gathered a fairly standard collection of offices in recognition of his new status: after some prodding, his civil service employer (the finance ministry) was induced to promote him to the first level of the senior grade of the civil service; he became a member of the Reichstag; and became head of the Reichsbund and Hauptamt.[29] However, none of these real or titular ranks prevented him from remaining an entirely peripheral figure in the serious battles over civil service politics. Despite the valiant efforts of his propaganda machine (which employed more officials than any other comparable Nazi organization) to foster an image of him as a seasoned member of the high councils of state, his real service to the regime was as a propaganda cheerleader. Yet because of the very volume of his speeches and publications, and the exceptional intensity of propaganda work in the Reichsbund, Neef has left an unusually full account of what was cultivated most extensively as the internally preferred image of civil servants in this period.

Under Hitler's slogan 'Erst deutscher - dann Beamter!'*, for

* 'First a German - then a civil servant!'

example, Neef addressed the civil service section of the 1933 party rally with a eulogistic account of what Nazism meant for civil servants. He claimed that 'National Socialism is nothing other than the purest, most loyal and most selfless service to nation and state, to perform which was the highest duty of the German civil servant'. The new Reichsbund, which replaced the 900-odd associations active in the Republic, would not be an interest group representing sectional demands, but would serve five main purposes: support for the government's campaign for national recovery and the creation of a true community; care for the civil servant's professional and moral values, on the basis of German tradition; the revivification of the meaning of the professional civil service as a part of the German community; concern for all civil service questions (here the ambiguous word Stand was used); and the professional and ideological education of civil servants.[30]   In a speech of 1934, characteristically hyperbolic language is used to show how the bad old ways of the Republic have been abandoned:

> 'Adolf Hitler has changed all that. He has
> returned the German civil servant to his people,
> he has taught the German people once again to see
> and respect its civil servants, he has
> re-awakened among non-civil servants, a sense of
> the necessity of the authoritarian work of the
> civil servant in the service of the state.'[31]

This was followed by invocations of civil servant and soldier as the two pillars of the state - the soldier as the 'bearer of arms' and the civil servant as the 'bearer of the will'. In general the comparison between civil service and armed service was a popular one in this kind of propaganda, being both more traditionally familiar and less hazardous than comparisons with the Party.[32]   The themes were discipline, respect, self-sacrifice, service to one's fellow-citizens; the problems of Party interventionism in and criticism of the civil service tended to be brushed aside with verbal formulae about unity of will and action, sometimes producing bizarre ideas: 'Adolf Hitler leads the Party and the Reich.   Just as he himself is indivisible, so also is the obligation that he imposes and that we all undertake';[33] or even 'The best and finest thing of all would be if everyone knew for himself how to act rightly as a National Socialist, without needing written instruction'.

Whether this banal pabulum actually satisfied its consumers is not a question that can be discussed here; but Neef and his colleagues did have the advantage, which they exploited, of access to an existing tone and tradition of language and sentiment. Civil servants were at least familiar with appeals couched in this kind of language, whereas for other classes and social groups Nazism had to invent its own authenticity. However, it is also true that this propaganda activity was relatively innocuous, ensuring that the most intractable political issues were dissolved into sentiment, purged of their dangerous meanings, their authors severely restricted in the scope and effectiveness of their work. The 'ordinary' civil servants and their representatives remained as marginal to their own fate as before - indeed, more so, for at least before 1933 the civil service associations had been seriously consulted by governments even if their interests were ultimately ignored.

49

4. Party attitudes towards the Civil Service.

The discussion of those groups well-disposed towards the civil service will have indicated that there were many Nazis, mainly with civil service experience themselves, who saw nothing intrinsically incompatible between the values of National Socialism and of the civil service. It was their experience of policy-making and practice after 1933 that shook them in this conviction. A parallel movement in reverse can be seen among those in the Nazi movement who began with a profound contempt for and hostility to 'bureaucracy' as such, and to the German civil service in particular. Obviously the 'anti-bureaucrat' groups had not developed the same strategic interest in the reform of the civil service before 1933, and for this reason do not lend themselves to the same kind of discussion as those who had. However, the development of their ideas and positions after 1933 is for the same reason more complicated; but to consider it fully would go far beyond the scope of this essay, since it would amount to a comprehensive history of the internal politics of the entire regime. The problem was that the experience of participation in government and administration obliged many to reconsider their blanket hostility, with total rejectionism being a luxury reserved only to those too remote from the day-to-day responsibilities of administrative work to have to grapple with it in practice. Yet even those faced with these problems often proved unable to reorientate themselves effectively to what was demanded by the actual exercise of power. It was as if 'politics' and 'administration' were thought of as two independent activities, with administration being assigned pejoratively to all that was most hated about the Weimar state.

Thus the rank-and-file Nazis' hostility to the civil service had two major targets: the Berufsbeamtentum as an elite institution, part of the 'anachronistic' class structure which the populist wing of National Socialism attacked with such virulence; and the 'petty bureaucrat', the self-important little official who represented the timidity and defeatism of the German state before 1933, and who allegedly obstructed the free-flowing dynamism of the Nazi-inspired German revival after 1933. This core hostility to and suspicion of the civil service was partly responsible for the delays in the organization of an NSDAP civil service section before 1933. The issue seems to have been raised early in 1930, and was followed by intermittent warnings from the Party's organizational centre against the creation of Standesgruppen representing sectional rather than national interests.[35] Although it was impossible to prevent unofficial groups from springing up, for example among railway officials in 1931, it was not until the spring of 1932 that official party sanction was given to the establishment of local groups for civil servants; by this time the calculation of electoral advantage must have played a part, perhaps also the need to impose central control over otherwise semi-independent groups claiming the authority of the party. Even so, there was no guarantee that the men (sic) nominally representing the civil service in the party would see themselves as defenders of their Stand. The local spokesman in Hamburg was allegedly quoted in 1930 (admittedly by a hostile source) as offering the following prospect for his colleagues under National Socialism: 'Civil servants will have to sit on their arses and keep their gobs shut' (language sic).[36] Crude though that is, it is only surprising in coming apparently from a civil servant; it represented an aspiration among ordinary Nazis which found expression after 1933 in a flow of abuse of civil servants in speeches and in the press.

Criticising or ridiculing civil servants is of course a national pastime in most countries, and was not unique to Germany in the 1930s. However, it was viewed with growing alarm by the civil service authorities, who by the later 1930s were taking the deterioration in official morale as evidence of a very serious crisis in the institution. Attacks on civil servants by party members at the time of the seizure of power, however, were already exposing the fragility of the political balances and alliances within the Nazi movement. At their most blatant and declaratory, the party's aims were summarised in Hitler's dictum at the 1934 party rally: 'Nicht der Staat befiehlt uns, sondern wir befehlen dem Staat' ('It is not the state that commands us, but we who command the state'). This was a statement that was both necessary at the level of political propaganda, but also meaningless at the level of practice. The sequel to it was evidently a renewal of attempts by local Party officials to issue orders direct to state authorities, followed by hurried reinterpretations of Hitler's words in order to reassert central authority.[37] The combination of propagandistic bombast and practical unreality was characteristic not just of Hitler, but of the terms within which the Nazi regime operated; and incidentally this episode makes an ironic footnote to Neef's observation about Hitler's indivisibility, quoted above. Tendentially, however, it also helped to crystallise the evolving distinction between men in the Nazi movement with access to conventional structures of power or responsibilities within existing institutions, and those who, to put it simply, had expected that a Nazi victory would mean the end of structures and conventions altogether. Because that expectation had formed such a strong theme before 1933, it could not be totally jettisoned thereafter, and remained one of the strongest elements of unreality among the tissue of illusions that sustained the regime.

The key illusion among the latter group was that the party ought to be able both to avoid attracting to itself the odium and the responsibilities of bureaucratic activity, and yet to establish and maintain effective political control over the machinery which would carry out these tasks. In the division between politics and administration, the party was to have the sole monopoly of politics but at the same time no formal responsibilities in the administrative sphere; it thus seemed to forget that it would need a machinery of enforcement itself. This was undoubtedly a vision that animated many Gauleiter, including that majority who also held state office as Reichsstatthalter or Oberpräsident, and that led them to claim verbally or in practice rights over the civil service in their locality. In the early years of the regime in particular there were numerous attempts by Gauleiter to force the appointment of 'politically reliable', men to civil service posts. Typical was, for example, a complaint by Gauleiter Weinrich in Kurhessen in September 1934 against the labour ministry's refusal to co-operate over a new appointment to the presidency of the Kassel state insurance office. As Weinrich warned in a letter to the Prussian interior ministry,

'I draw your attention to the fact that the [Nazi] movement insists on this appointment. Furthermore I must emphasise as a matter or principle that the movement does not expect to be

> treated as the labour ministry is doing, because
> this vital post must at all costs be filled by a
> National Socialist...Even tthe labour ministry
> might be aware of the fact that the primacy of
> the Party is to be secured...'[38]

What this meant locally is illustrated by an example from the other side: a report from the Oberpräsident of Magdeburg, Ulrich, also in 1934, that experienced and trained civil servants were unwilling to take up the demanding post of Landrat (the state representative at local level) for fear of being forced into bearing an impossible dual responsibility to state and to Party.[39]

Interventions of this kind were never stamped out throughout the life of the regime, and were paralleled by continuing party interference in the local execution of policy and by attempts to control civil servants' more private behaviour (such as the notorious and absurd bids to encourage marriage and childbearing).[40] This failure to control local and regional Party officials was not surprising: it was characteristic of the centrifugal nature of the Nazi movement itself; while the top level of Nazi leaders – men like Goering, Hess, Bormann, Ley, R. Wagner – gave their less illustrious comrades many lessons in how to conduct internecine power struggles. The question of whether and how far the civil service should be Nazified was thus never resolved, partly because the meaning of the term was never clarified. This itself derived from the initial and fundamental impossibility of resolving the relationship between party and state at the vital intermediate level of norm-setting. There were many verbal bids to solve it, some of which we have noted above, and even these were often deeply resented by old-school civil servants, for whom rhetoric was almost a way of life. Thus a disaffected Landrat, Dr Reschke of Recklinghausen, writing in 1941, morosely rejected the assumption that to the NSDAP alone fell the honour and task of leadership – for, as he pointed out, the Landrat and the Bürgermeister had their own long and independent tradition of being 'leaders of men'.[41] At the level of day-to-day practice, some forms of working relationships were obviously established, but these were brittle and unpredictable. Moreover, frictions, appeals, attempts at reconciliation, bids to preserve power positions, temporary and insecure alliances – all this took up an inordinate amount of official time and energy.

Deficiencies of this kind could not fail to be noticed by all those involved in administrative work, whatever their formal status. A series of memoranda, conferences and internal debates from about 1936 (when Gauleiter Sauckel produced the first of his two major memoranda on the problems of the regional administration) testifies to the dissatisfaction of the party's officials at the chaotic administrative procedures and at their lack of control over the civil service, which they regarded as linked problems. In the early 1940s, the critique of Germany's government was expressed in a spate of writings and meetings, the questions having by then become the more urgent because of the additional tasks imposed by war and conquest. To a large extent, all this amounted to a belated recognition that the questions of civil service and administrative reform had been approached in too ad hoc a fashion in 1933, and had been foreclosed on prematurely as soon as politically sensitive conflicts threatened to come out into the open.

However, there was still no unanimity about possible solutions; and by
this time too there were even fewer channels of communication between
the members of the regime than there had been in 1933: years of
suppressed conflict had dispersed the regime into a series of isolated
and embattled units. The question of civil service formation was quite
directly addressed in such writings as Gauleiter Roever's 1941 memo on
the party,[42] or in Hans Frank's 1940/1 lectures at the Munich
'Institute for State Practice' which he had founded in order precisely
to conduct research into the newest methods of administration.[43]
These and some similar (partly anonymous and fragmentary) writings
represent the clearest analyses we have of the Nazi regime's recognition
of its own failures. It can't be claimed that these texts had a wide
contemporary resonance, except as evidence of a general atmosphere of
complaint. Nevertheless, they make instructive reading because of their
concessions – reluctant or disguised – to exactly that bureaucratism and
professionalism which had been at such a discount in and before 1933:
qualities the absence of which was now being held at least partly
responsible for the failure of National Socialism to maintain its
political authority in the state, and for the disintegration of the
administration into unco-ordinated and overlapping bodies.

It would be an exaggeration to end by claiming that the
absence of a coherent civil service policy in 1933 was solely
responsible for the overall political crisis of the regime to which
these texts are a testimony. Nevertheless, they present a significant
confirmation of the parallel evidence from within the 'pro-civil
service' camp that the civil service itself was undergoing a crisis of
morale and effectiveness. Even if the latter camp chose to put more
emphasis on the decline of a traditional institution and the distress of
its members, and chose also to exploit this sense of crisis for its own
purposes, we can at least see that the problem was not simply
manufactured by them for sectional ends. It will remain a matter of
speculation whether the German state would have been torn apart by its
own tensions if it had not been militarily defeated: certainly, its
resilience was quite astonishing. Speculatively, however, a new battle
of bureaucracies, between Bormann's semi-state structure, and Himmler's
SS police system, was already underway as Germany's military collapse
was looming.

I am deeply grateful to Jeremy Noakes for his advice in the drafting of
this essay.

Notes

(I have kept source references to a minimum, in order to avoid
overloading the footnotes; I have also tried where possible to give
prominence to works available in English.)

1. Enclosure in a letter from the Education Ministry to the President
of the Examination Commission for Higher Administrative Civil Servants,

53

23 April 1936; Bundesarchiv (=BA) R 115/517.

2. A full set of references here would require a bibliography to
itself. The best accounts of the literature are Dietrich Kirschenmann,
'Gesetz' im Staatsrecht und in der Staatsrechtslehre des
Nationalsozialismus (Berlin, 1970), and Michael Stolleis,
Gemeinwohlformeln im nationalsozialistischen Recht (Berlin, 1974), both
of which include extensive quotations from contemporary writings, and
full bibliographies.

3. Internal note from Frick to state secretaries Pfundtner and
Grauert, 23 December (1935); BA R 18/5564.

4. This series begins with a note from Bormann to Lammers, 11 August
1941, and the documentation on the sequel is in the same file, BA R 43
II/583. A reminder of the instructions was issued on 17 February 1942,
evidently as part of an unsuccessful bid by Lammers to recover authority
for his chancellery by means of something very similar to a revival of
the cabinet system; BA R 43 II/958.

5. Otto Kirchheimer, 'The Legal Order of National Socialism', in
Studies in Philosophy and Social Science IX (1941), p.467.

6. See, for example, the essay by Jeremy Noakes in this volume. A
more general survey and literature review is Hans Mommsen's excellent
'National Socialism: Continuity and Change', in Walter Laqueur (ed.),
Fascism. A Reader's Guide (Harmondsworth, 1979), pp.151-192. The best
short German survey of the debate is Peter Hüttenberger,
'Nationalsozialistische Polykratie', in Geschichte und Gesellschaft 2
(1976), pp.417-422.

7. See Jane Caplan, '"The imaginary universality of particular
interests": the "tradition" of the civil service in German history', in
Social History 4, ii (1979), pp.299-317.

8. Arnold Köttgen, Das deutsche Berufsbeamtentum und die
parlamentarische Demokratie (Berlin and Leipzig 1928), p.1.

9. The phrase derives from an article by Hugo Preuss, 'Die
Improvisierung des Parlamentarismus', published in 1919; quoted in
Gerhard Schulz, Zwischen Demokratie und Diktatur, Vol 1 (Berlin, 1963),
p.21.

10. See Hans Mommsen, 'Die Stellung der Beamtenschaft in Reich, Länder
und Gemeinden in der Ära Brüning', in Vierteljahrshefte für
Zeitgeschichte xxi (1973), pp.151-165; and his more recent and
comprehensive 'Staat und Bürokratie in der Ära Brüning', in Gotthard
Jasper (ed.), Tradition und Reform in der Deutschen Politik.
Gedenkschrift für Waldemar Besson (Frankfurt, 1976), pp.81-137.

11. These quotations are taken from Martin Broszat, Der Staat Hitlers.
Grundlegung und Entwicklung der inneren Verfassung (Munich, 1969),
pp.301-302. An English translation of this excellent study is
forthcoming.

12. Wilhelm Frick (ed.), Die Nationalsozialisten im Reichstage

1924-1928 (Munich, 1929), p.60.

13.   Wilhelm Frick, (ed.), and revised by Curt Fischer, Die
Nationalsozialisten im Reichstag 1924-1931 (Munich, 1932), p.155.

14.   F. Dickman, 'Die Regierungsbildung in Thüringen als Modell der
Machtergreifung', in Vierteljahrshefte für Zeitgeschichte xiv (1966),
p.462; Donald R. Tracey, 'The Development of the National Socialist
Party in Thüringia 1924-1930', in Central European History 1975,
pp.25-50.

15.   See Hans Fabricius, 'Der Reichsleiter Dr. Frick', in Hans Pfundtner
(ed.), Dr. Wilhelm Frick und sein Ministerium (Berlin, 1937), p.180.

16.   Strasser's views as reported by the Prussian interior ministry to
the Berlin police presidency, 27 March 1931; BA NS 26/122.

17.   Deutsche Verwaltung, 20 November 1934.

18.   See references in note 6 above; also Jane Caplan, 'Bureaucracy,
Politics and the National Socialist State', in Peter D. Stachura (ed.),
The Shaping of the Nazi State (London, 1978), pp.234-256.

19.   See the file on Fabricius held by the Berlin police presidency
before 1933; BA NS 26/1345.

20.   Information about Stuckart is compiled from documentation held by
the Berlin Document Center (=BDC), from BA R 43 II/1154, and from the
Geheimes Staatsarchiv (=GStA) Rep.90/883. See also E.N. Peterson, The
Limits of Hitler's Power (Princeton, 1969).

21.   Deposition by Kettner, Institut für Zeitgeschichte (Munich)
Zeugenschriften 1093.

22.   See note 23 above; also a note from the interior ministry to
Lammers, 2 April 1943, asking that Stuckart's request be refused, as his
ministerial work was indispensable; BA R 43 II/1136c.

23.   See his essay, 'Partei und Staat', in Wilhelm Stuckart and
Gottfried Neesse (eds.), Partei und Staat (Vienna, 1938), p.10.

24.   From an unpublished essay 'Grundgedanken zur Neuordnung des
Ausbildungsganges der höheren Verwaltungsbeamten', typescript dated 5
August 1940 (first 2 pp. missing), p.6; Nachlass von der Schulenburg (I
am grateful to Professor Hans Mommsen for allowing me access to this).

25.   Ibid., p.11.

26.   For Schulenburg, see Albert Krebs, Fritz-Dietlof Graf von der
Schulenburg. Zwischen Staatsraison und Hochverrat (Hamburg, 1964). See
also Hans Mommsen, 'Social Views and Constitutional Plans of the
Resistance', in Hermann Graml et al., The German Resistance to Hitler
(London, 1970), pp.55-147.

27.   'Das preussische Erbe und der nationalsozialistische Staat',
typescript dated March 1938, p.17; Nachlass von der Schulenburg.

28. Reprinted in Hans Mommsen, <u>Beamtentum im Dritten Reich</u>, pp.146-149.

29. Information on Neef compiled from his BDC files, and those on Sprenger; some further details taken from R 18/2132 and 5524.

30. Reported in <u>Nationalsozialistische Beamten-Zeitung</u>, 5 September 1933.

31. <u>Der Beamte im nationalsozialistischen Führerstaat</u> (Berlin, 1934), p.4.

32. For example, Neef's <u>Das Soldatentum des Deutschen Beamten</u> (Berlin, 1936). Not surprisingly, the comparison became even more common during the war.

33. <u>Das Soldatentum des Deutschen Beamten</u>, p.9.

34. Hermann Neef, <u>Die politische Forderung an den Beamten in Recht und Gesetzgebung</u> (Berlin, 1937), p.6.

35. Information here compiled from the following sources: BA NS 22/361; BA Sammlung Schumacher file 218; BA NS 26/vorl.1411.

36. Quoted in Helmut Klotz, <u>Nationalsozialismus und Beamtentum</u> (Berlin, 1931). Klotz was, however, a renegade from the NSDAP, whose reliability as a source is therefore suspect.

37. For an attempt at exegesis, see the minutes of the sitting of the Prussian Ministerial Council, 16 October 1934, in which Göring emphasised that Hitler's words did not give Party offices any authority to interfere directly in governmetal work: rather, they were to be read as meaning that once trusted Party members had been placed in influential posts in the administration, Nazi ideology would become the basis of all administrative work; GStA Rep.90/2339.

38. See exchange of correspondence in GStA Rep.77/3.

39. This was among a series of extracts from a number of Oberpräsidenten situation reports, sent to Hess by Göring, 31 August 1934; copy in BA R 43 II/1263.

40. In April 1937 Gauleiter Schwede-Coburg of Pommern tried to ban the promotion of any unmarried civil servant over the age of 25; copy of his instructions, 10 April 1937, in BA R 22/20789. This was foiled by the intervention of the interior ministry, which not untypically started its own initiative on the subject of marriage and childbearing, rather than simply countermanding Schwede-Coburg's unauthorised move; see its instructions to subordinate offices, 14 December 1937, GStA Rep.90/2340. Hitler eventually vetoed the whole business; see documentation in Rep.151/3026. Behind all this lay some entirely (at the time) serious questions about the low fertility of civil servants, and its relationship to the long duration of their training.

41. Copy, dated April 1941, in BA R II/703.

42. Extracts are printed in Noakes and Pridham, op.cit., pp.259-264.

43. Reprinted as Hans Frank, Die Technik des Staates (Berlin, Leipzig and Vienna, 1942).

3. Popular Opinion in the Third Reich

IAN KERSHAW

'Public opinion', in the sense of opinion publicly held and expressed, was after 1933 almost wholly that of the Nazi regime, or at least of rival sections within the ruling elites. Yet the survival of an inchoate ground-swell of spontaneous, unorchestrated attitudes beneath the surface of the apparently monolithic unity, which was the regime's propagated image, was recognised by the regime itself, which set up its own apparatus to test, probe and keep check on opinion, if only to be able to steer propaganda more effectively. In distinction to 'public opinion', a term by and large applicable only to societies where there exists a plurality of freely and publicly expressed opinion, it seems sensible to designate such attitudes and responses - unquantifiable, often unspecific, diffuse and ill-coordinated, but real for all that and held by large if indeterminate sections of society even though not normally publicly articulated - as 'popular opinion'.

This paper attempts to indicate the main lines of development of some central aspects of popular opinion during the Third Reich, especially in the period before the war. It concentrates on those areas of Nazi policy which produced the highest level of consensus and those which resulted in notable conflict or dissension in order to bring out different 'layers' of opinion; it seeks to cast light on the relative effectiveness or failure of the attempt to manipulate and mould opinion, and the extent to which the regime was dependant upon a plebiscitary base of support or could develop a wide degree of autonomy from the attitudes of the mass of German society in pursuit of its goals. Any attempt to analyse the relationship between the Nazi regime and German society must consider at least four crucial 'layers' of opinion: the personal standing of Hitler within the framework of domestic and foreign policy; the response to the demands of Nazi social and economic policy; the effect of the conflict between Church and State; and finally, reactions to the persecution of the Jews. Each of these is considered below, though it is not possible in this article to do more than summarise conclusions drawn from a mass of evidence which has been fully documented and analysed elsewhere.

After 1933, when the curtain falls on free and open expression of opinion, the development of popular attitudes towards Nazism can only be impressionistically reconstructed. Interpretation can never take full cognisance of the multiplicity of individualistic motives for supporting or rejecting a particular measure or policy. Conclusions must remain, for the most part, tentative and suggestive. Yet, if we are to penetrate at all the relationship between the Nazi leadership and the German people, it seems important to establish, at least in broad terms, those areas in which Nazi policy alienated considerable sections of society and those which succeeded in winning wide popular support for the regime. This can only be achieved by deducing general patterns of opinion from sources – mainly confidential reports on opinion and morale by agencies of the regime and reports smuggled out by opposition groups to the exiled leadership of former left-wing parties – all of which have a strong internal bias, are subjective appraisals of the situation, and allow no possibililty of quantification. The weaknesses and complexities of such material have been thoroughly examined elsewhere. Despite the difficulties of interpretation, however, such sources do allow a fairly nuanced outline of the main strands of popular opinion in the Third Reich.

1. The Personal Popularity of Hitler.

In the Reichstag election of 5 March 1933, held against a backcloth of the assault on the Communists and in the heady atmosphere of the 'National Revival', just under one in two Germans (43.9%) voted for the Nazi party and a further 8% for the German Nationalists, the Nazis' coalition partners. Aboveaverage support for the NSDAP came chiefly from the rural areas of the protestant north and east, whereas the Nazis were still unable to destroy the electoral blocks of the Left and of political catholicism, which left them relatively weak in most large cities and in the predominantly catholic regions of the south and west. However, the NSDAP achieved spectacular gains in particular in catholic rural areas, where the Nazis were often able to treble or even quadruple their vote compared with the previous election of November 1932.

It seems highly likely that already by the March election Hitler's personal popularity was running considerably ahead of that of the NSDAP. Without the evidence of contemporary opinion polls this remains a surmise, but the speed with which his popularity grew in the following months suggests strongly that not all of those who voted against the NSDAP in March 1933 were opposed directly to Hitler. Much of what he seemed to offer in spring 1933 appealed to far more than just hard-core Nazi support. In this fact lay the prospect of a massive extension of Hitler's prestige if he could demonstrate some success in tackling what were seen to be national problems, if he could transcend his image as party-leader and become accepted as a national leader. More than all else, far more than the slight improvement in the economic prospects in the first weeks of his chancellorship, Hitler's growing stature as a national leader was due to the ruthlessness with which his government attacked the parties of the Left. The selective wave of terror unleashed against those widely regarded in bourgeois circles as the enemies not of the Nazis but of Germany itself was massively popular and brought Hitler much acclaim.

This was one area in which the regime could, in its early days, build upon a ready consensus. In two other important respects, despite the social, ideological and political cleavages in German society at the beginning of the Third Reich, there existed outside the third or so of the population which had been attached to the left-wing parties – largely, though not exclusively, in the industrial working class – a broad if vague consensus. First, the belief was widespread that strong leadership was needed to transcend class and sectional interests, to master Germany's economic, political and social crisis, and to create a new unity and base for future prosperity. Secondly, there was a general feeling not only that Germany had been wronged in the Versailles settlement, but that the country was threatened by hostile nations on all sides. A government which was seen to aim at restoring Germany's strength, and with it salvaging and rebuilding national pride at the same time as providing greater national security, had a strong possibility of gaining wide popular support. Both areas of greatest potential consensus, inner unity and outward strength, were reflected in the popular conception of Hitler.

The greatest success of Nazi propaganda, as Goebbels himself realised, was in creating the Führer myth. As a consequence, the popular image of Hitler after 1933 became increasingly dissociated not only from that of the party, but even from the government itself. The gulf between myth and reality, between Hitler as he was and Hitler as he was imagined to be, was enormous. Thus, for example, the summary shooting of the SA leadership in June 1934, for which Hitler took full responsibility, won him massive acclaim. His action was widely interpreted not as an affront to morality, but as a moral act in itself carried out by the representative of elemental popular justice, extirpating corruption and immorality in high places and intervening to restore order. In contrast to the arrogance, high-handedness, incompetence, scandal, and corruption which characterised the image of the Nazi Party's functionaries increasingly from 1933, the simple life-style and high ideals of the Führer, extolled by Goebbels' propaganda, seemed to stand out in sharp relief. In addition, Hitler's constant avowals of deep religious belief and his interventions to calm the situation in critical moments of struggle with the Church made him appear to be the pious defender of Christianity against its atheistic assailants within the party. Removed from the arena of everyday politics, therefore, Hitler's popularity, based on the Führer myth, provided an important source of legitimation for the regime. Successes could be attributed solely to his genius, grievances were levelled at the failings of his subordinates and of the party functionaries.

The popular conception of Hitler was, therefore, that of the Führer kept in ignorance of events by his underlings, and yet of the unerring great statesman who, despite his lofty status, was in touch with what the regime-jargon called 'the healthy sentiments of the people' and understood instinctively the point of view of 'the little man'. This Hitler image, on the one hand a conscious creation of the propaganda machine, on the other the unconscious creation of the expectations and needs of society, held appeal for all social groups. If the main centres of Hitler's undoubted massive popularity remained the lower middle classes, which had always formed the backbone of Nazi support, the reports of left-wing sympathisers reaching the exiled SPD leadership in Prague admit the attachment shown in all circles of German society, even among the working-class, to the person of the Führer and the consequences this had for attempts to undermine the popularity of the regime as a whole. Whatever the grievances, Hitler tended to be exempted from criticism, often no doubt to express political conformity but often too, it seems, genuinely and sincerely, even by groups such as catholics who were otherwise not slow to demonstrate their disaffection with party and regime.

Most important of all, Hitler's popularity rested upon his apparent achievements. Within the framework of domestic policy this

amounted to the belief that Hitler alone had provided the leadership
necessary to master Germay's economic crisis and to restore order,
authority and prosperity. Even if, as we shall see, opinions on the
'economic miracle' of the Third Reich varied widely, the achievements of
the regime, by which everyone understood the achievements of Hitler
seemed, superficially at least, to be extremely impressive. Those
dissenting could be decried as inveterate grumblers, incapable of being
satisfied. In any case, whatever the economic dissatisfaction which
remained, for many the miseries of the depression were too recent to be
forgotten. This all amounted to the fact that the argument against the
Nazi view that the Führer had rescued Germany was difficult to put
convincingly, except perhaps for the bulk of the industrial working
class which was paying the lion's share of the price of the economic
recovery.

Above all, however, it was in the realms of foreign policy
that Hitler's achievements seemed incomparable. Here too his popularity
was based upon a total misconception of his aims, but here also he could
rely upon the maximum level of acclamation for the accomplishment of an
international standing for Germay which was hardly conceivable at the
time of his accession to power.

Hitler's foreign policy successes were genuinely popular.
They accorded with pre-existing resentments and aspirations widely-held
in Germany before Hitler came to power. Hitler seemed to be the
exponent of national, not simply National Socialist, values, and to
represent Germany's completely just claims for national sovereignty
based upon the overturning of the terms of Versailles and Locarno. As
national triumphs, the reoccupation of the Rhineland, the unification
with Austria and, to a lesser extent, the 'homecoming' of the
Sudetenland, won the acclaim of most Germans, even those antagonised by
Nazi anti-church policies or disenchanted with Nazi economic and social
policy. The way in which opposition groups within the Wehrmacht were
disarmed by Hitler's 'triumph' at Munich in 1938, because of the
impossibility of acting against such a popular leader, is well known.
Left-wing opponents of the regime also recorded how much harder the
string of diplomatic coups made their task of trying to alienate people
from the regime.

With the exception of a small minority, German popular
opinion with regard to foreign policy was dominated by the fear of
another war, and, as Hitler himself realised, his popularity was due in
no small measure to the fact that his triumphs had been achieved without
bloodshed. The dread of another conflagration, especially prevalent
among the older generation which remembered the horrors of the First
World War, became especially apparent during the Sudetenland crisis in
the summer of 1938, when some confidential reports even speak of a 'war
psychosis' among the population, and the utter lack of enthusiasm for
the war in 1939 is documented in all accounts. Yet despite the
unpopularity of the war itself, Hitler's own popularity was never
seriously threatened before the invasion of Russia. Although now the
most constant theme of popular opinion was the longing for the end of
the war, the stream of cheap and easy German victories dispelled fears
and seemed to confirm Hitler's genius in leading Germany out of the
abyss to the pinnacle of European dominance. Furthermore, Nazi
propaganda had undoubtedly been very successful in emphasising that the

war had been forced upon an unwilling Germany by the western allies, and once the war had begun, the propaganda was even more easily able to identify Hitler with national goals. It was now increasingly difficult for those less than wholly convinced by the Nazi leadership to avoid allegations of unpatriotic behaviour through their show of hostility towards Nazism. A marked decline in Hitler's popularity only began with the failure of the Blitzkrieg in Russia in the winter of 1941. Thereafter there are clear signs of growing disenchantment with Hitler's leadership and increased readiness to see his policies as the root cause of the disaster facing Germany. His popularity nose-dived after Stalingrad, though it had fallen seriously before the catastrophe. However, astonishing reserves of popularity remained. Even towards the end of the war, many prisoners of war taken on the western front continued to show a high degree of loyalty to Hitler, though in the last phase of the war the sustained defiance of the Germans owed less to idealism than to the level of terror and the certainty of immediate retribution for 'defeatism' or expression of anti-Nazi feeling.

The pseudo-integration of German society which resulted from the popular acclaim for Hitler, falsely conceived as it was, not only disarmed critics of the regime within the Reich, but also played a fundamental role in legitimising the Nazi regime in the eyes of the outside world. The plebiscitary base of Hitler's policy, his personal popularity, and the popular support for his major achievements were recognised by foreign observers and played a part in forming the attitude towards Germany's new rulers which crystallised into Appeasement. To the outside world the unity of leadership and people trumpeted by Nazi propaganda seemed at least to approximate to reality. The periodic but extremely short-lived bursts of euphoria which accompanied the diplomatic triumphs were, however, mere interludes in the formation of popular opinion. A more continuous impact was made by issues, less spectacular in themselves but affecting directly the everyday lives of the population. In the response to Nazi social and economic policies there was far less consensus and far more conflict than we have been witnessing so far.

2. Economic-based Discontent

Many Germans in the Third Reich were, like foreign observers, impressed by what appeared to be a Nazi social revolution, above all a revolution in attitudes which made possible the new society founded on achievement not privilege. The abolition of workers' parties and trade unions was, they could argue, more than compensated by the benefits provided for workers by the creation of 'Strength through Joy', improved facilities in factories, and above all by the removal of the scourge of unemployment. The peasantry, it seemed, had benefited from the Nazi regime to an extent they had done under no previous government. The middle classes and business circles could profit from the revitalised economy. The younger generation were catered for by the new discipline of the Hitler Youth organization, and for the remaining poor and less fortunate members of society there was the Winter Aid scheme and the various forms of assistance administered by the NS-Volkswohlfahrt. This was, of course, the propaganda picture, and it was not without impact inside and outside Germany. The propaganda success rate was, however, much higher among those who were not immediately affected by the Nazi

social policies they were praising than among the direct
'beneficiaries'. Despite the 'brave new world' suggested by Nazi
propaganda, deep social divisions and sources of serious discontent
remained scarcely concealed by the veneer of the harmonious
Volksgemeinschaft and were mainly countered by sheer repression.

The first clear signs of a growth of adverse opinion, chiefly
a reflection of economic-based discontent, occurred in 1934. The
initial optimism about the economic policies of the new government,
especially the work creation programme, was already giving way by the
spring of 1934 to growing criticism, most clearly apparent among social
groups which had previously been prominent in their support for Nazism.
Numerous reports point to widespread disillusionment and disappointment
in sections of the Mittelstand (lower middle class) about the failure of
the regime to eliminate the unfair competition for small businesses
which came from department stores and consumer associations, about the
lack of available credit, the compulsory contributions for party funds,
the lack of assistance for the tourist trade, and so on. The motives
were mainly personal, self-interested and material. A swing in opinion
away from the regime was also apparent to all observers among the
peasantry, another backbone of Nazi support before 1933. The provisions
of the Reich Inherited Farm Law of September 1933 were one cause of
conflict and growing ill-feeling in rural areas. Apart from a
prevailing sense of lack of freedom to dispose of their property or to
provide for their children as they had been accustomed to do, the
removal of farm property from the market had the practical consequence
that the supply of rural credit all but dried up. In addition there was
growing resentment among wide sections of the peasantry at the
increasing intervention of the Reichsnährstand (Reich Food Estate) in
the running of their farms and in the control of the marketing of
agricultural produce, which invited frequent unflattering comparisons
with the coercive economy (Zwangswirtschaft) of the war years. Reports
spoke of a serious loss of confidence among the peasantry, and some
commentators even inferred that the mood was as bad as it had been in
1917 and 1918.

This was certainly a gross exaggeration, and it would be a
mistake to overemphasise the extent of adverse opinion in 1934. Even
hostile sources, such as the reports on conditions in Germany reaching
the exiled SPD leadership (or Sopade as it now called itself), pointed
out that apart from the limited nature of many of the grievances the
regime could rely upon great reserves of support, especially among the
younger generation, and that many critics admired Hitler even when they
castigated the party. The materially-based disillusionment in lower
middle-class circles was, claimed these reports, devoid of political
significance: fear of communism and 'lack of political education', as
one report put it, was sufficient to ensure the further approval of the
Nazi government by the petty bourgeoisie, despite their economic
complaints. Passivity and carping trivial criticism were seen by Sopade
informants as the main characteristics of popular opinion. In their
view, the inner weakness of the regime's opponents could be ascribed to
ignorance, fear, lack of 'political will', and the atomisation of
society so that not even 'group opinion' remained intact. Even leaving
aside the massive coercive powers of the regime and its support from
hundreds of thousands of beneficiaries of Nazism, the Sopade arrived at
a pessimistic assessment of the divisions of opinion even among those

antagonistic towards the NS-Regime:

> 'The weakness of its opponents is the strength of
> the regime. Its opponents are ideologically and
> organisationally weak. They are ideologically
> weak because the great mass are only discontents,
> grumblers whose dissatisfaction arises solely
> from economic reasons. That is especially so
> among the Mittelstand and the peasantry. These
> social strata are least of all ready to fight
> seriously against the regime because they know
> least of all what they should fight for...The
> anxiety about bolshevism, about the chaos which,
> in the opinion of the great mass in particular of
> the Mittelstand and the peasantry, would follow
> on the fall of Hitler, is still the negative mass
> base of the regime.
>
> Its opponents are organisationally weak, for it
> is in the essence of the fascist system that it
> does not allow any organisational gathering of
> its opponents. The forces of "reaction" are
> extraordinarily split...The working class
> movement is still split into socialists and
> communists...The attitude of the church opponents
> of the regime is not united. Their struggle is
> evidently for the most part directed at improving
> the position of the churches within the
> regime.'[1]

This perceptive report indicates the main weaknesses of
popular opinion, in terms of political action, throughout the Third
Reich. Nevertheless, economically-based disillusionment among
substantial sections of the population was to deepen considerably in the
following years.

A new peak of unrest was reached in the winter of 1935-6,
when a critical shortage of key foodstuffs - butter, fats, eggs and meat
- was compounded by farmers holding back their produce in the hope of
selling at inflated prices. The sharp rise in food prices - one report
spoke of a 33% rise in the price of meat and 25% in the price of white
bread in some areas since 1933 while wages had remained stable or had
even fallen somewhat because of short time[2] - meant a substantial drop
in real wages and genuine hardship especially for the working population
of industrial regions. Indeed, unlike 1934, when discontent had been
most vehemently expressed by farmers and the Mittelstand, the most acute
criticism in 1935-6 came from the industrial working class, the section
of the population towards which the Nazi leadership was most sensitive.

Serious unrest among the working class in particular was
registered with concern in reports of the Nazi authorities from all
regions. They recorded an increase in criticism of the Nazi leadership
and new signs of life among opposition groups, whose verbal agitation
was falling on fertile ground in many factories and especially on
motorway construction sites which since 1933 had been centres of
anti-regime feeling. A sharp rise in the number of cases of workers

being taken into 'protective custody' or indicted before the Special Courts in some parts of Germany reflects the increased dissatisfaction. Bitter criticism was voiced of working conditions, of the Labour Front and the Nazi party, of the lack of social justice in the Nazi state shown by the contrast between the miserable wages of the workers and the fat salaries and company dividends of the bosses, and of the waste of money on Nazi representative buildings when the housing shortage was so acute and living standards falling. Nazi reports spoke of 'a growing ill-feeling against Government and Party'[3] which was making itself felt among workers. Less prosaically, Sopade reports from big industrial districts like the Ruhr, Saxony and Berlin recorded 'feverish unrest in all sections of the population' and a mood close to the point of explosion, saying: 'One can ask whom one wants to, all sections of the population are against the system. One can only wonder that this government can still exist.'[4]

This was clearly an over-reaction. Other Sopade reports were anxious not to overestimate the significance of adverse popular opinion on the economic question, and to stress again the divided nature of opinion, the naivety of many views which drew no ideological or political lessons from their discontent, and of course the fear, intimidation and atomisation which prevented any organization of opinion. One report called the widespread dissatisfaction 'a pure matter of feeling without political reflection', and another argued that it would be mistaken to regard the general discontent as direct hostility to the regime, pointing out the ready compliance with orders despite the criticism and the frequent cases in which 'people complain very extensively about conditions and then again shout the loudest when they are fired with enthusiasm by Nazi speakers in some rally or other.'[5]

In terms of their productive capacity and key position in the economic drive, the two social groups whose morale most concerned the Nazi leadership in the last years before the war were the peasantry and above all the working class.

Reports from all sources agree in their estimation of widespread and growing peasant discontent between 1936 and 1939, as agriculture was sacrificed on the altar of rearmament and the pressures upon farmers intensified accordingly. Above all, it was the labour shortage crisis which brought demoralisation and discontent to the countryside between 1936 and 1939. The SD spoke, in its annual report for 1938, of a 'mood close to despair' among farmers. The drain of rural labour to the better paid jobs in the armaments industry 'gave the peasant the feeling of being crushed and produced a mood which turned partly into resignation and partly into an attitutde of downright revolt against the peasant leadership'[6]. The Reich governor of Bavaria added, in a long report compiled in spring 1939, that 'the lack of labour has reached indescribable limits...The mood of the peasantry has reached boiling point.'[7]

There was, however, a deep ambivalence about peasant political opinion in the Third Reich. Those who most vehemently demanded state intervention to deal with the supply of labour were those who continued to decry oppressive state interference in regulating agriculture through the 'coercive economy' (Zwangswirtschaft).

Furthermore, despite its disadvantages, the Nazi state had given the peasant price stability and sales guarantees which hedged him against the effects of a slump. It was not a wholly one-sided picture. On the one hand, therefore, there was remarkably frank expression of great discontent, especially by older farmers, but on the other hand there were serious divisions of opinion among the peasantry so that the discontent could never develop into a serious political challenge to the regime. Against the deep economic disillusionment had to be balanced, as Sopade reports pointed out, the acute fear and hatred of communism among the peasantry, heightened through Nazi propaganda: between the devil and the deep blue sea, many feared 'that Bolshevism will take away their land and property and prefer to come to terms with the Nazis who only half-expropriate them'.[8]

Measured solely in terms of real wages, the position of industrial workers - especially those in the relatively well-paid armaments industry - improved between 1936 and 1939. However, the view that higher wages and the benefits of Nazi social policy won over workers to Nazism in these years would hardly be tenable. The critical labour shortage and the drastically accelerated tempo of work under the Four Year Plan, putting workers under growing physical and psychological stress, produced a serious intensification of industrial conflict which necessarily had a bearing upon political opinion. Increased militancy on the shop-floor was reflected in a sharp increase in work stoppages or short strikes in big industrial regions, in absenteeism and indiscipline, and in a rapid turnover of the labour force as workers left without notice for positions offering better pay and conditions. The regime's answer was to restrict worker mobility, to conscript labour for important military projects, and generally to step up repression in order to enforce work discipline.

The degree of repression to which industrial workers, more than any other section of society, were subjected meant that they were especially reserved and careful about expressing their political views. Resignation rather than defiance characterised the outward stance of most workers. In fact the Sopade reports, which were keen to seize upon any expression of working class hostility towards the regime, emphasised repeatedly the difficulties of arriving at a generalised interpretation of worker attitudes towards Nazism, stressing factors such as the composition of the work-force, labour relations in the factory and the approach of the local party offices which could affect political attitudes.[9] In a report just before the war, the Sopade pointed out again the overwhelming impression of exhausted, sullen apathy made by so many workers simply going through the motions, resigned in the force of absent alternatives. Contrary to the view of some of its reporters, the Sopade concluded that falling production in, for example, the mining industry was a result above all of physical exhaustion and not of deliberate sabotage or overtly politically motivated action. Even accepting the internal bias of the reporting, it points strongly to the effective neutralisation rather than winning over of the working class by Nazism. The success of Nazism, the report ended, lay in the atomisation of the working class and the destruction of its leadership, which had previously been able to overcome differences and weld disparate groups together. Nazi repression had deepened the differences which had always existed: 'those who used to think, still think today, and those who were not then used to think, think now even less: only

that the thinkers are today no longer able to lead the
non-thinkers.'[10]

Practically every section of the population could find
grounds for discontent with its own particular position in the society
of the Third Reich. Reports from the immediate pre-war years suggest
disenchantment, rooted in the personal material interests of the
individuals or groups concerned, among lower civil servants and white
collar workers, sections of the free professions and bourgeoisie, and
even among the youth. In each case the gap between expectations from
Nazism and the reality of the Third Reich shaped the feelings of social
injustice. Discord, disillusionment and discontent were present on all
sides, but little of it needed to be taken seriously by the regime.
Complaints among civil servants, for example, about low pay, overwork
and interference by the party in their domain meant little in political
terms since despite grumbles they were invariably prepared to do the
extra work necessary and generally sympathised with some if not all aims
and policies of the regime. Furthermore, all social groups contained
those who had benefited directly from Nazism, so that there was seldom
even unanimity of feeling let alone organizational possibilities within
specific groups.

Nazi social policies resulted in widespread and often
far-reaching criticism and antipathy. However, opinion was split into
its component parts. There was little unity of attitude, even among
groups like the peasantry and the working-class, and the economic-based
discontent of one group could not easily be conveyed to other groups
with quite different socio-economic interests. The lack of opportunity
to organize, channel, direct and lead opinion meant that there was no
possibility of gathering a coalition of interests, of overcoming the
group-based antagonisms and welding together a broad horizontal critique
of the regime, let alone an ideological front of opposition.

Though we cannot enter here into the development of
socio-economic influences upon the formation of political opinion during
the war, it is evident that the social divides and group-specific
attitudes which we have outlined in this section continued to exist and
were even more sharply accentuated by the tensions and pressures which
war imposed on civilian life. Though events at the front naturally
exercised a dominant influence on the shaping of opinion, the euphoria
accompanying the victories of the first phase of the war was very
swiftly dissipated and replaced by the social and material discontent
which, heightened by the restrictions and deprivations which eventually
fell upon German society, became magnified until the bitter taste of
military defeat and the horrors of the bombing united it into a broad
front of hostility to the NS-Regime.

Contrary to the views of those who see in the Third Reich a
social revolution, if one of forms and subjective attitudes more than of
the substance and structure of society, Nazi social and economic
policies seem merely to have deepened and hardened the already existent
class- or group-determined attitudes of the peasantry, the industrial
working class and the bourgeoisie, and under the superficial unity of
the German nation at war, the basic class and group divisions and
antagonisms remained largely intact.

3. The Impact of the Church Struggle

Among the substantial sections of the population closely attached to the major religious denominations, no single aspect of Nazism created as much antagonism or shaped attitudes towards the NS-Regime as decisively as the attack on the Christian churches. We can merely point here to four occasions when the churchgoing population showed open opposition to Nazi measures, in order to demonstrate the depth of feeling aroused by the attack on Christian institutions and values but also the extremely limited nature of the hostile popular opinion.

When Bishop Meiser, head of the Bavarian Lutheran Church, was removed from office and placed under house arrest in autumn 1934 almost the whole of protestant rural Franconia rose in protest. Angry letters, resignations from the party, demonstrations, mass assemblies and deputations to the prime minister of Bavaria took place. Alarming reports reached the authorities of the rebelliousness of the population on the issue and its consequences for the prestige of party and state. Four deputations, each claiming to speak for up to 70,000 Franconian peasants, minced no words in pointing out to the prime minister the extent of the bitterness, even in this area where Nazism had thrived before 1933.[11] However, although opinion was certainly radicalised, it affected no other sphere of Nazi politics. The protest was limited to the restoration of Bishop Meiser and to fending off the challenge to the protestant church in Bavaria. It took place in an area of solid Nazism, and many alte Kämpfer of the party took part in it. Though the party itself undoubtedly lost face in the conflict, Hitler, whose intervention to end the dispute seemed to mark a victory of moderation over nihilistic radicalism, was wholly exempted from criticism. Although it was theoretically possible for a specific grievance to spill over into a general condemnation of the regime, it did not do so on this occasion. Unrest over the church issue coexisted quite easily with the national values which not only the bulk of the Franconian population supported, but which were also held by influential 'opinion-leaders' among even those ranks of the clergy belonging to the 'Confessing Church' wing of protestantism.

In catholic regions of Germany – Bavaria, the Rhineland, the Mosel valley, Baden, the Palatinate and substantial parts of Silesia and Westphalia, in all accounting for about a third of the population – the church struggle took on the shape of a war of attrition running between 1935 and 1939 and then flaring up again in 1941. Two incidents will show the full force of popular opinion in the face of the assault on catholic institutions, traditions and values, and point to parallels with the case we have just seen in the protestant church.

The removal of crucifixes from schools by order of the regional government offices in the catholic districts of Oldenburg in 1936 and in Bavaria in 1941 contained the ingredients which could convert tension and antagonism into a mass revolt. The removal of the very symbol of Christianity from the schools was the spark from which the church struggle flared up into open, widespread resistance to the implementation of government decrees. The wave of civil disobedience in both cases, involving petitions, protest letters, mass meetings, school strikes and even a demonstration of coordinated car-horn hooting, presented the Nazi authorities with a situation which, as in the protestant case, the conventional weapons of coercion were powerless to control. Both in Oldenburg and in Bavaria the authorities eventually gave in amid much loss of face, and popular opinion had scored in each case a notable, if limited, victory.

Despite the deep antagonism, spectacularly expressed, the narrow confines within which hostile popular opinion operated are again clearly demonstrated. The issue concerned only the withdrawal of the decrees ordering the removal of the crucifixes, and the replacement of the crosses in the schools. As soon as this was done, peace and quiet returned. The restricted criticism of policies affecting only denominational issues had no relevance to groups outside the ranks of churchgoers, and furthermore was perfectly compatible with a set of values which extolled authoritarian government, the assault on marxism, and anti-liberal, corporatist and nationalist attitudes common to most German catholics and Nazis alike. In the Bavarian example, defence of the Church in 1941 was coupled with strong support for the Führer's fight against Bolshevism raging on the eastern front and both here and in the earlier Oldenburg case, too, Hitler seems to have been widely exempted from blame. If the Nazi regime had held to the letter of the Concordat of 1933, as by and large the Mussolini government kept to the Lateran Agreement of 1929, it is extremely unlikely that the catholic population would have casued it much trouble.

The final example of hostile popular opinion forcing the Nazi government to amend its policies occurred in a much more fundamental issue than the denominational questions we have been considering. This concerned the 'Euthanasia Action', introduced by secret written order of Hitler in autumn 1939 and accounting for the deaths of some 70,000 mentally and physically handicapped before being brought to a halt two years later following pressure articulated by the hierarchies of both Christian denominations.

The regime had taken prior soundings about possible negative reactions of the Churches and their followers before commencing the 'action', but evidently miscalculated the response to the seeping out of disturbing rumours about the extermination of the mentally sick. The very secrecy of the 'action', as later with the 'Final Solution of the Jewish Question', points to the scepticism of the regime about the response of popular opinion. It was also proof of the limited extent to which the central racial-eugenic element of Nazi ideology had gained ground in popular consciousness.

The intended complete veil of secrecy was impossible to maintain, and within a year disturbing rumours about the fate of the mentally sick were in circulation. In the vicinity of the sanatoriums where extermination was taking place, such as Hadamar in Hesse and Grafeneck in Württemberg, the local population was well aware of what was happening. Harrowing scenes were encountered in other places when the inmates of mental asylums were being forced into the grey buses which everyone knew would be taking them to their certain death. Party leaders became increasingly aware of the necessity to allay public anxiety. Letters of enquiry, of complaint, and of protest poured into party and government offices. Leading Nazis began to question the wisdom of proceeding in this way, without any published law on the

matter. There was alarm and unrest in the provinces, and the Nazis were
prepared to take notice. Numerous bishops and other members of the
clergy had written protest letters about the 'action'. Now, as public
anxiety grew, the hierarchies were prepared to bring their opposition
out into the open, verbally and in print. The most famous protest was
that of Bishop Galen in his celebrated sermon on 3 August 1941, in which
he publically attacked euthanasia as a breach of the fifth commandment.
He followed this up with another broadside in a pastoral letter eleven
days later. The Nazi leadership was urged to hang Galen. Goebbels
pointed out, however, that

> 'if anything were done against the Bishop, the
> population of Münster could be regarded as lost
> to the war effort, and the same could confidently
> be said of the whole of Westphalia'.[12]

The only course of action was, in his opinion, not to challenge the
church as long as the war lasted. Instead, Hitler gave the order to
halt the 'euthanasia action'.

Even here the framework of oppositional opinion was limited.
In some instances Nazis whose loyalty was beyond reproach were involved,
and the disturbing feature for some protesters was not the destruction
of life itself, but that there was no law officially permitting the life
to be taken. Outside the ranks of churchgoers, especially catholics,
opinion on the justification of euthanasia seems, in fact, to have been
quite divided, as the varied responses to the Nazi propaganda film on
euthanasia, 'I Accuse' ('Ich klage an') suggested.[13] Moreover, even
for the church leaders who had articulated the deep unease in the
population, the euthanasia issue was not related to a total assault on
the Nazi state. Some of the central Nazi policies were regarded not
only as legitimate, but to be applauded. Bishop Galen himself, in the
pastoral letter just mentioned, regarded the invasion of Russia as the
beginning of a crusade in 'defence against the Bolshevik threat to our
people'.[14] Galen's hatred of the Nazi regime needs no stressing, but
the ambivalence of his views is just as self-evident. Many of the
values which he cherished were those of the regime he was castigating.
This points to the deep ideological confusion among church leaders, and
those they were supposedly leading during the Third Reich.

4. Reactions to the Persecution of the Jews

Economic factors and the church-state conflict had, as we
have seen, an obvious and direct impact upon popular opinion. It is
hard, however, to escape the conclusion, based upon a great deal of
evidence from a variety of sources, that for the mass of the German
population the 'Jewish Question', which lay at the centre of Hitler's
own political ideas and those of his movement, was largely a matter of
secondary importance, even indifference.

The first three years of Nazi rule were punctuated by
sporadic violence against Jews, especially in the antisemitic waves of
spring 1933 and summer 1935, linked to the attempt to force Jews out of
the economy. The Nazis found it, however, extraordinarily difficult to
convince the German people of the necessity of the 'boycott movement'

and of breaking its economic ties with Jews. Material self-interest rather than principled objection was no doubt the dominant motive in most cases for continuing to patronise Jewish shops or dealers, but the open violence used by Nazi mobs did to some extent provoke sympathy with Jews and antipathy towards the Nazi party, whose image was tarnished by methods abhorrent to bourgeois liking for 'peace and order'. Reports from many parts of Germany point to the repulsion felt by 'decent' Germans at the treatment of the Jews and at the distasteful gutter antisemitism of the Streicher variety. Such feelings were particularly expressed in catholic regions and among sections of the bourgeoisie influenced by liberal humanitarian values and traditions. Nevertheless, even sources hostile to the regime admit that the sheer volume of anti-Jewish propaganda was beginning to make itself felt and that growing numbers of people were coming to approve of the aims of Nazi anti-Jewish policy, even where they condemned the particular methods employed to implement that policy. A sign that antisemitism was gaining ground despite the instinctive repulsion towards the brutal assaults on Jews was the fourfold increase in the circulation of Streicher's pornographic antisemitic newspaper Der Stürmer in the first ten months of 1935.[15]

The basic lack of interest of the population in the 'Jewish Question' showed itself in the muted reactions to the promulgation of the Nuremberg Laws in September 1935. Many reports do not even mention the laws, which appear to have passed by much of the population almost unnoticed. The tenor of other reports suggests that the laws were taken more or less for granted, or were welcomed primarily in the hope that by giving the whole question a legal framework the violent 'wild' antisemitism of the summer would be ended.

Between the promulgation of the Nuremberg Laws and the summer of 1938 it would not be going too far to suggest that the 'Jewish Question' was almost totally irrelevant to the formation of opinion among the majority of the German people. When, in February 1936, a Nazi official was murdered by a young Jew in Switzerland, there was scarcely a ripple of interest in the population as a whole. The manipulation of 'popular anger' in the 'Jewish Question' is as blatant for its non-appearance in 1936 as it was for the pogrom allegedly erupting from this 'anger' in November 1938.

Extensive evidence of reactions to the November pogrom, the 'Reichskristallnacht', indicates that this nationwide night of violence unleashed by Goebbels as the 'spontaneous answer' of the German people to the murder of a Legation Secretary by a young Jew in Paris a few days earlier alienated popular opinion rather than won it over to support for Nazi anti-Jewish measures. Rejection of the pogrom was again most widespread in the relatively urbanised, more densely settled catholic south and west, and among the intellectuals and the liberal and conservative bourgeoisie. The SD summarised from its own standpoint the reaction to the pogrom among the bourgeoisie by stating:

'The actions against the Jews in November were very badly received...From a basic liberal attitude many believed that they had openly to stand up for the Jews. The destruction of the synagogues was declared to be irresponsible.

People stood up for the 'poor repressed Jews'.[16]

However negative the instant reactions to 'Reichskristallnacht', the pogrom had no lasting impact on popular opinion. It was the one and only time in the Third Reich that the 'Jewish Question', cornerstone of Nazi ideology, was in the forefront of people's minds and at the centre of popular opinion. Within a few weeks even this event had receded into the background of people's consciousness. It was not something which had concerned them directly, and had been perpetrated against a tiny and basically unloved social minority. The Nazis were finding it difficult to turn the latent dislike of Jews, widespread in Germany as in most European countries, into active hatred, but the latent antisemitism was sufficient to provide no obstacle to the implementation of Nazi racial policies.

During the war years interest in the 'Jewish Question' declined still further. The deportations passed off apparently little heeded by the population. Most people seem to have asked little and cared less about the fate of the Jews. The war, its worries and deprivations, dominated opinion. The Jews were out of sight and out of mind. Knowledge of shootings and atrocities in the occupied territories was widespread, and rumours about extermination circulated. Details, in particular about the systematic gassing programme in the camps, appear, however, to have been largely unknown.

Despite an unceasing barrage of antisemitic propaganda, the last two years of the war saw the German population preoccupied less than ever with the 'Jewish Question'. Party propagandists reckoned that hundreds of thousands of young Germans now scarcely knew 'what the Jew is'. For the young, 'the Jew' was only a 'museum-piece' to be viewed with curiosity, 'a fossile wonder-animal,...a witness of bygone times'.[17] This was testimony at one and the same time to the progress of abstract antisemitism, and to the difficulty of keeping alive the hatred of an abstraction.

In its attempt to infuse the German people with a dynamic, passionate hatred of the Jews, the Nazi propaganda machine was less than successful. Except on isolated occasions when directly confronted by the 'Jewish Question', especially in November 1938, Germans seldom had Jews on their mind. Popular opinion on the 'Jewish Question' ranged in a wide spectrum from the small minority of paranoid Jew-baiters through a broad band of varying degrees of intensity, where abstract acceptance of the racial policy was coupled with rejection of the most overt forms of inhumanity, ending in another minority still imbued with a deeply Christian or liberal-humanitarian moral sense, whose value-system provided the most effective barrier to the Nazi doctrine of racial hatred. The constant barrage of propaganda failed to make the Jews the prime target of hatred for most Germans, simply because the issue seemed largely abstract, and unrelated to their own specific problems. The result was, for the most part, widespread lack of interest in the 'Jewish Question'. Amid the widespread apathy, however, the 'dynamic' hatred of the few, whose numbers included some of the leaders of the Third Reich, among them Hitler himself, could flourish.

V   Conclusion: the Nazi Regime and German Popular Opinion

Seldom has a government placed so much store on the control and manipulation of opinion as did the Nazi regime. Yet, despite some notable propaganda successes, steerage was incomplete. A 'popular opinion' independent of the Goebbels-directed 'public opinion' continued to exist beneath the monolithic uniformity of the Third Reich.

Since the regime was so anxious to manipulate opinion, and since it was in a fairly good position to monitor opinion, especially during the war through the regular reporting of the SD, it is reasonable to ask to what extent popular opinion influenced Nazi policy, whether in fact it had any impact at all on the Nazi leadership, or whether the regime could ignore it altogether.

We have seen instances in this paper where the regime, in sensitive areas of domestic policy such as the church struggle, gave way to the force of popular feeling, most notably in the halting of the 'euthanasia action' in 1941. The regime's apprehension about stirring up unrest in the working class, rooted in the memories of 1917-18, also limited its manoeuvrability. Contrary to much weighty advice, Hitler was unwilling to depress living standards by cutting consumer spending in the pre-war years, and anxious to avoid imposing too many demands on the civilian population during the war. In 1938 Hitler himself banned any rise in food prices because of its likely effect on morale, and just after the beginning of the war the attempt to reduce wages and abolish various bonuses was abandoned following worker protest and the threat of disruptive unrest in major industrial regions.

Hitler was, in fact, sharply aware of the value of plebiscitary support. He spoke of the function of the plebiscites which followed major foreign policy successes in terms of their effect at home as much as abroad, and of the need for constantly renewed psychological mobilisation of the people. He also expressed on more than one occasion his apprehension about a drop in his popularity and about the danger of future instability should the run of successes not be continued. His sensitivity to unrest led him to intervene directly in instances, such as in the church conflict, where it seemed the evident unpopularity of specific measures was endangering confidence and morale. It is even alleged that he threatened to send <u>Gauleiter</u> Wagner, the Education Minister of Bavaria, to Dachau if he were to repeat the crass and unnecessary alienation of the population which his decree ordering the removal of crucifixes from Bavarian schools had caused.[18]

Yet it was distinctly morale rather than opinion which really concerned Hitler and the Nazi leadership. This was shown most clearly in the middle of the war when, at a time that the SD reports were falling into increasing disfavour on account of their negative and defeatist tone, a distinction was demanded by Nazi leaders between comments on the 'mood' (<u>Stimmung</u>) of the population and evaluation of the essential 'attitude' or 'bearing' (<u>Haltung</u>) of the people. It was claimed that although the 'mood' was obviously depressed as a result of bombing raids, rationing and other privations of war, the basic 'attitude' of the German people remained positive and unwavering. Hitler made his own feelings clear in one of his Table Talk monologues in 1942 when, in the circle of his intimates, he declared: 'If what

people always say were decisive, everything would long since have been
lost. The true attitude of the people lies, however, much deeper and is
based on a very firm inner bearing.'[19] Such views were given support
by the very one-sided reports coming in from party offices. The
increasingly negative tenor of the SD reports, on the other hand, was
more than the leadership could stand: the central digest of reports
coming in from all parts of the Reich was halted in July 1944.

Opinion as such, therefore, was unlikely to sway Hitler or
the Nazi leadership either where it did not suggest a dangerous drop in
morale, or where it ran counter to fundamentals of Nazi policy. In two
areas above all popular opinion was practically without relevance.
These were foreign policy and the persecution of the Jews, the two areas
central to Hitler's own Weltanschauung.

Even in parliamentary democracies foreign affairs are
probably less influenced by popular opinion than any other sphere of
politics. Yet, indirect though it was, the impact of opinion on British
and French foreign policy in the 1930s or the effect of popular pressure
on the USA to withdraw from Vietnam in the 1960s was considerable. The
overwhelming majority of Germans in the 1930s dreaded another war, yet
by 1939 they were involved in one. The rapid fall in Hitler's
popularity in the later war years was testimony to the growing
recognition that his policies were responsible for the horrors and
miseries of war. By 1944, perhaps even earlier, a very large number of
Germans would have been prepared to cut their losses and to surrender in
order to bring about an end to the destruction. This had no impact
whatsoever on the regime's leadership, which was determined to continue
the struggle even if this meant the eventual total destruction of the
German people.

The regime's autonomy in the 'Jewish Question' was equally
clear. The terror, harassment and the hounding of Jews out of German
society was not carried out in response to the demands of popular
opinion, though neither was it hindered by any vociferous opposition to
the measures. Indifference characterised popular attitudes. The
extermination of Jews in the occupied eastern territories clearly
indicates the autonomy of the regime from popular opinion: in
recognition of the fact that the German people were not ready to
participate in the mass slaughter of Jews, Himmler told his SS leaders
in the middle of the war that this was a 'never to be written glorious
page of our history', whose secret 'it was better to carry to the
grave'.[20]

Nazism contained something for most Germans; it also
contained much that alienated, in different ways, very many Germans.
Nazi ideology was so diffuse, and included so many aspects which were
largely a recasting of orthodox bourgeois values that, by emphasising
these values, the regime could build upon a considerable consensus
already present in wide sections of society. However, Nazism painted
over rather than eliminated the divisions within German society, which
remained reflected, however darkly, in the formation and expression of
opinion. Despite the extravagant claims made by Goebbels and the
propagandists, attitudes were formed in the Third Reich as in every
society by a multiplicity of factors, only some of which were directly
controllable by the regime, and which involved shadings of opinion

dictated by class or group allegiance, individual preferment or benefit from the political system, denominational affiliation, geography, type of community relationships, nature of local political leadership, and strength of previous political, ideological and religious attachment.

Far from a neat division into pro- and anti-Nazi attitudes, an examination of popular opinion during the Third Reich produces a complex mosaic of overlapping but disparate pieces. The verticalisation of opinion - the reduction of it into its component parts - was a crucial consequence of <u>Gleichschaltung</u> and the elimination of any political apparatus which could build and organize cross-sectional, horizontal opinion. The fracturing or atomisation of opinion also accentuated the ambivalence of political views - rejection of parts of Nazism, but approval and acclamation of other crucial aspects, and the inability or unwillingness to draw general ideological conclusions from specific instances of antagonism. The important, multifaceted substrata of hostile or antagonistic opinion therefore coexisted with, or were neutralised by, the transcending consensus of support for national policy, the identifying focus of which was Hitler. Significantly, as the 'positive' integration of the population declined sharply from the mid-war onwards coercion and repression had to be increased proportionately.

Popular opinion could make itself felt only in the most muted way during the Third Reich. The autonomy which the Nazi government gained, and which led to war and genocide, arose out of the vacuum created by the German people's abdication, between 1930 and 1933, of its democratic rights. These rights alone are the safeguard of a measure of influence for public opinion in shaping government policy and in controlling those who wield power.

Notes

The research upon which this article is based was supported by a grant from the Alexander von Humboldt-Stiftung.

[1] Wiener Library, "Deutschland-Berichte der Sopade" (henceforth "Sopade"), 26.6.34, p.B.22-3 and see also pp.A.1-22.

[2] Geheimes Staatsarchiv (GStA), Munich, MA 106 682, report of the Regierungspräsident of Schwaben, 7.9.35.

[3] GStA, MA 106 682, report of the Regierungspräsident of Schwaben, 9.10.36.

[4] "Sopade", 16.10.35, p.A.3; 12.11.35, pp.A.2,5.

[5] "Sopade", 16.10.35, pp.A.1-2.

[6] Bundesarchiv Koblenz (BAK), R58/1096, Fol.9-10.

[7] GStA, Reichsstatthalter 563.

[8] "Sopade", 18.9.37, p.A.40.

[9] "Sopade", 14.4.39, pp.A.85-6; and see also 10.10.38, pp.A.79-80.

[10] "Sopade",12.7.39, pp.A.77, 83-4.

[11] GStA, MA 107 291.

[12] Jeremy Noakes and Geoffrey Pridham (eds.), Documents on Nazism 1919-1945 (London, 1974), pp.308-9.

[13] Heinz Boberach (ed.), Meldungen aus dem Reich (Neuwied, 1965), pp. 207-11,

[14] Heinz Boberach (ed.), Berichte des SD und der Gestapo über Kirchen und Kirchenvolk in Deutschland, 1934-1944 (Mainz, 1971), pp.570-1.

[15] "How popular was Streicher?" (no author), Wiener Library Bulletin, V/VI (1957), p.48.

[16] BAK, R58/1094, Fol. 109.

[17] Cited in Marlis G. Steinert, Hitlers Krieg und die Deutschen. Stimmung und Haltung der deutschen Bevölkerung im Zweiten Weltkrieg, (Dusseldorf, 1970), p.259.

[18] See Edward N. Peterson, The Limits of Hitler's Power (Princeton, 1969), p.219.

[19] Henry Picker, Hitlers Tischgespräche im Führerhauptquartier 1941 bis 1942 (Stuttgart, 1963), p.206.

[20] International Military Tribunal, XXIX, pp.145ff., Hans Buchheim et al., Anatomie des SS-Staats, (Olten 1965), I, p.329.

4. Class Harmony or Class Conflict ? The Industrial Working Class and the National Socialist Regime 1933-1945

STEPHEN SALTER

Introduction

The long-established socialist tradition in Germany, the size and structure of the industrial working class, the extent of the organization of this class in socialist trade unions and parties, all suggest that the nature of the relationship between the National Socialist regime and the industrial working class should be a central concern of all historians investigating the impact of Nazi rule on the class structure of German society. Yet in many respects, the historiography of the working class in Germany during the Nazi period is much more meagre than that of the working class during the Wilhelmine period. There are no comparable studies of the ways in which workers developed organizations and a class consciousness as a consequence of their industrial experience, nor of the considerable obstacles which stood in the way of working class unity. To a certain extent, this historiographical gap may be attributed to the paucity of the source material: the sources on which 'labour historians' normally rely to build up a picture of workers' activity - reports and minutes of trade union meetings and a socialist press, for example - are absent for the period after May 1933. Thus, historians have been forced to rely on official reports - and face the problems of the ideological 'filter' through which the authorities saw labour questions. Moreover, in the light of these problems with source materials, it is exceptionally difficult to build up an accurate picture of working class political consciousness: this must be largely inferred from the ways in which workers behaved - though even here the historian is confronted by serious problems as a consequence of the very considerable constraints on the extent to which workers could register their protest against working conditions, or political decisions, in the face of the omnipresent threat of coercion. In the case of the Third Reich, it is even more difficult than usual to study 'labour questions' in isolation - the extent of the Nazi claims to have re-ordered society along non-class lines, the importance to the regime of establishing a pattern of industrial relations relatively free of conflict if rearmament were to go ahead at full speed, and the difficulty of tracking down decision-making processes in the Third Reich, all preclude this.

It might be best to begin with a definition of what I understand by the term 'working class'. By this, I mean manual industrial workers, largely organized in trade unions and normally associating themselves politically with the German Socialist Party

(SPD), the German Communist Party (KPD), or, perhaps less frequently, with the catholic 'Centre' Party (<u>Zentrum</u>). I exclude white-collar salaried workers, and workers in essentially 'non-industrial' occupations – agricultural workers and workers in small artisan workshops, for example.

I. The Nazi Party and the Working Class before 1933

Hitler frequently claimed that he had entered politics in order to provide a nationalist alternative to the Marxist social-democratic parties he had seen in Vienna before 1914, and the winning-over of the industrial working class for nationalism was a central tenet of Nazi social thinking from the earliest days of the party. It now seems clear that the Nazis appreciated the significance of the November 1918 revolution much more than they have hitherto been understood to have done. Hitler interpreted the revolution in terms of on the one hand, urbanisation, the destruction of 'German' values, and the alleged increase in the influence of German Jews in public life: and, on the other, in terms of the 'stab in the back' – the army had been betrayed by striking workers, who had been led astray from their naturally patriotic outlook by the influence of criminals, Jews and Marxists. This domestic political weakness rather than any military considerations, Hitler believed, was the main cause of Germany's defeat in the First World War. If Germany were to be restored to world-power status, the 'inner front' must be secured; that is, the industrial working class must be won over to support the aims of a nationalist regime. Thus, the integration of the working class into a 'national community' (<u>Volksgemeinschaft</u>) became one of the principal aims of the Nazi movement before 1933, and later of the Nazi regime.

How did workers respond to this policy? After the reestablishment of the Nazi party in February 1925, Nazi activists in the urban centres of north and west Germany sought to break the electoral hold of the SPD, KPD and <u>Zentrum</u> over the industrial working class. Yet this attempt – largely associated with the Strasser brothers, Goebbels, Krebs and others – was largely unsuccessful. Although the Nazi party could claim some successes in the industrial centres of Berlin, and in some of the industrial cities in the Rhineland, Westphalia, Saxony and Thuringia, these were of minimal significance in both electoral and membership terms. This is hardly surprising. In the socialist and catholic trade unions and parties, the working class had organizations which, as a consequence of their long practical experience, organisation and solidarity, commanded its allegiance. Only the KPD formed a partial exception to this, largely as a consequence of its relatively recent formation and tempestuous history. The influence of the SPD and <u>Zentrum</u> in both national and regional (<u>Land</u>) government and administration (especially in Prussia, in the case of the SPD), and the improvement in wages and living standards and the introduction of social welfare measures by the Weimar governments after the stablisation crisis of 1923-4, all reinforced the loyalty of industrial workers to their traditional parties. The Nazi party could offer workers little but slogans, and its rabid nationalism was, if anything, a handicap when appealing to workers whose political consciousness, transmitted particularly through the SPD and the socialist trade unions, was heavily influenced by the opposition of the principles of 'nation' and 'class', as a consequence of the close

connection between nationalism and reactionary political goals before
1918. The other appeals made by the Nazi party – based on denunciation
of the Versailles treaty, which was alleged to be responsible for much
unemployment, hostility to 'finance capital' (but <u>not</u> to 'productive'
i.e. industrial capital), assurances that 'workers of the hand' would
receive as much respect in the future Third Reich as 'workers of the
brain', a pseudo-egalitarianism, and accusations that the functionaries
of the SPD and the socialist trade unions had 'sold out' to the Weimar
'system' – appear to have made little impact on industrial workers.

Moreover, the development of the German economy and German
society, and the changing electoral constituency of the Nazi party after
1928, made it increasingly unlikely that the Nazis would win any
significant support from the industrial working class. The social
groups which most clearly formed the basis of Nazi electoral support
after 1928/9 – the 'old middle class' (<u>alter Mittelstand</u>), and to a
lesser extent, the 'new middle class' (<u>neuer Mittelstand</u>) – effectively
shaped the form and content of Nazi propaganda: Nazi propaganda
advocated reduction of taxation, higher prices for food products,
restrictions on consumer and department stores, a reduction in wages and
social services. Such propaganda was hardly calculated to make much
appeal to industrial workers, and the Nazis must have confirmed the
suspicions of many workers when they reestablished the traditional
connection between nationalism and the Right in German politics through
their alliance with Hugenberg's conservative party (against the Young
Plan) in 1929. This helps to account for the fact that between 1930 and
1932, the already strong inverse correlation between the manual variable
in the industrial sector and the Nazi vote became even more pronounced:
while the correlation between the unskilled manual variable in
handicrafts and small-scale manufacturing and the Nazi vote (which had
been significant between 1924 and 1928) collapses. Unemployed workers
did <u>not</u> vote Nazi: if workers were radicalised by their experience of
unemployment, they voted Communist – unemployment, especially in areas
with a high concentration of industrial workers, is a much stronger
correlate of the KPD vote than of the Nazi vote. Nor was industrial
working class membership of the Nazi party ever significant. The
membership patterns correspond, by and large, with the electoral bases
of the party. Moreover, the party 'trade union', the National Socialist
Factory Cell organization (NSBO), made little headway among industrial
workers. Established in 1928, the NSBO was originally intended to
function solely as a propaganda organ: and yet, by 1932, it was to be
found supporting strikes and claiming a prominent role for itself in the
social-political arena after the party came to power. The apparent
radicalisation of the NSBO was a consequence of its experience in
dealing with industrial workers and attempting to win their trust and
support: yet it was regarded with suspicion by the leadership of the
Nazi party, which was anxious not to alienate the conservative business
establishment. The membership of the NSBO before Hitler's appointment
as Chancellor peaked in late 1932 at 300,000 – compared with 5.8 million
workers who were organized in the socialist and catholic trade unions.

II. The Destruction of Working Class Organizations during the 'Seizure of Power':

Thus, when Hitler was appointed Chancellor in January 1933,
the Nazi party had clearly failed to win the support of the industrial

working class. Yet the foreign policy aims of the regime demanded the integration of the industrial working class into the Volksgemeinschaft. Having failed to win the workers away from the SPD and KPD through electoral propaganda and party activity before 1933, the regime was committed from the outset to the repression of the workers' movement and the destruction of working-class representative institutions - the socialist and communist parties, and the trade union movement. Yet the precise means by which this aim was to be achieved were not clear: rather, the regime was subject to considerable pressures which shaped the form its policies took, especially pressures from the local and regional activists of the party and the SA. Thus, at the beginning of March 1933, the Reich Labour Minister, Seldte, had plans drawn up whereby the power of the socialist trade unions in economic and political life was to be gradually reduced. Yet after the Reichstag fire (28 February 1933), the wave of local Party and SA activity directed against the Left had begun to force the regime's hand: so that Seldte's plans were redundant almost before they were drawn up. The employment of the SA as auxiliary police to break the organization of the KPD (especially in Prussia) had initiated this process. By mid-March, the unions could barely function in many large German cities, following the attacks on trade union officials and the occupation of trade union buildings in early March, spearheaded by the SA, SS and NSBO. By the end of March, the NSBO felt compelled to draw the attention of the Prussian ministry of the interior to the fact that it was necessary to permit the trade unions to make welfare payments to their members - the union structure had been so badly shaken by the SA terror that even this elementary function was threatened. The SA and NSBO also took it upon themselves to occupy the places of socialist and communist representatives on the factory councils. The changing situation may be gauged by the fact that in the Berlin factory council elections of early March 1933, the socialist unions were still able to retain the bulk of their support: but by early April 1933, the NSBO with 30% of the vote had already gained a relative majority in the factory council elections in the Ruhr (after the SA had proclaimed that union candidates would not be allowed to take their places as delegates if elected), and the membership of the NSBO rose rapidly in summer and autumn 1933. The promulgation of the 'Law on Shop Representatives and Economic Associations' of 4 April 1933, merely rationalised a state of affairs brought into being by the terroristic methods of the SA.

At first, the regime was alarmed at the way in which the SA was pre-empting its campaign against the socialist unions. Yet when it became clear that the campaign was producing no organized opposition from the trade unions, Hitler, Goebbels and Ley (the Reich organization leader of the Party), decided to exploit the situation to settle the trade union question quickly. Thus, in late April plans were drawn up for the take-over of the unions. Following a massive rally on 1 May 1933, at which Hitler spoke, emphasising the sympathy of the regime for manual workers, the majority of the offices of the trade unions were occupied (2 May 1933). To a considerable extent, this coup represented an attempt by the regime to regain the control of the situation which it had lost during March and early April: the majority of the offices occupied on 2 May had in any case only been able to function under the 'supervision' of the SA and NSBO for several weeks. Moreover, there was no clear idea as to the kind of industrial order which was to replace the unions.

Perhaps the most striking feature of the Nazi 'coordination' (Gleichschaltung) of the representative institutions of the organized labour movement is the lack of resistance this encountered. The reasons for this relative passivity on the part of the working class and its organizations, are largely to be sought in the effects of the economic crisis of 1929-33 on the German labour movement. By 1932, national income was 40% lower than it had been in 1929, and one-third of the working population was unemployed. The economic crisis hit industrial workers particularly severely. By 1933, 40% of all male industrial workers were unemployed – compared with 13% of all white-collar workers. Moreover, the state unemployment insurance scheme collapsed under the strain of having to cope with over 6 million (registered) unemployed: and the effects of mass unemployment extended to employed workers. Of those fortunate enough to have retained their jobs, at least 16% were working short time. The condition of the labour market combined with enactment of the Brüning government's wage reductions and the rising cost of living, reduced the real wages of industrial workers by about 15%: to which a further 3% fall in real terms must be added for increased tax and insurance contributions. The fall in retail turnover in groceries, clothing, beer and tobacco (of the order of 30%) confirms this. Workers were forced to work harder to keep their jobs, and found themselves competing with one another in the wake of mass dismissals. Thus, productivity in the coal-mining industry rose and reached its inter-war peak. It was inevitable that the unions would suffer in this situation: about two-thirds of their members were either unemployed or working short-time, and employment was greatest in precisely those sectors of industry which were best organized. The unions consequently suffered massive financial and organizational damage. Mass unemployment made it difficult for unions to represent their members effectively. Although they succeeded in opposing the attempt of the von Papen government to rescind the binding nature of collective wage agreements, they could not prevent the steady decline in wages, mass dismissals and the reorganization of production techniques. Employers paid no attention to their demands that the available work be divided amongst the greatest possible number of workers in order to avoid unemployment wherever possible. Faced by a massive pool of potential strike-breakers, many union leaders rejected the possibility of a political strike outright. In any case, it was by no means certain that all union members would be willing to risk their jobs by participation in a strike: this applied particularly to workers in public employment whose participation would be essential to the success of any such strike. This partly helps to explain the passive legalistic stance of the SPD leadership, the increasing concern of the central trade union organ, the ADGB, simply to preserve the trade union apparatus – pathetically reflected in the petition sent by union leaders to Hitler, Hindenburg, and various Reich Ministers protesting against the outrages of the SA in March-April 1933, all of which were filed unread.

The working class movement was also hampered by the divisions between the SPD and the KPD which were largely a consequence of the fear of the former that the KPD threatened to draw away the more radical elements in the SPD, and the subordination of the KPD to the Comintern and its consequent pursual of the 'ultra-left' tactic, namely denunciation of the SPD as objectively 'social fascist'. The SPD was in a particularly helpless situation: the policies for which it had struggled – the expansion and reform of state social welfare policy, in

particular – were now threatened by the economic crisis. Following
pre-Keynsian economic theory (i.e. a deflationary policy), the SPD felt
unable to oppose cuts in welfare expenditure: on the other hand, the
radicalisation of its members at the regional and local levels by the
economic crisis, prevented it from taking any share in government and so
modifying the impact of the cuts. The political limbo which the SPD
occupied before 1933 goes a long way to explain its passivity in the
face of the Nazi terror of spring 1933.

III. Labour Legislation and the Creation of the German Labour Front (DAF):

By May 1933, the KPD could no longer function as a political
party: and the SPD was on the verge of collapse. The socialist 'free'
trade unions had been 'coordinated', and the liberal Hirsch-Duncker
unions were to merge with the newly-formed German Labour Front
(Deutscher Arbeitsfront, DAF). The Concordat between the Vatican and
the Nazi regime, and the consequent dissolution of the catholic trade
unions and the Zentrum, completed the hegemony of the Nazi regime in the
social sphere by July 1933. The week following the coup against the
trade unions in early May, had been characterised by a hectic debate
about how they were to be replaced, the details of which are not clear.
On 6 May, Ley announced the formation of a new organization, the DAF.
Once again, the establishment of this organization should be seen in
terms of the desire of the Reich leadership to retain control of the
social situation – in this instance, to thwart the ambitions of the NSBO
to replace the trade unions. The activities of the NSBO in putting
pressure on (mainly smallscale) employers to make wage concessions and
to replace social-democratic workers with unemployed Nazis, also forms
the background to the 'Law on Trustees of Labour' (Reichstreuhänder der
Arbeit) of 19 May 1933, whereby the ultimate authority for wage
regulation was handed over to thirteen labour trustees, each responsible
for a particular district and subordinated to the ministry of labour.
The trustees gradually assumed control over wages and working
conditions: their powers were more clearly defined in the 'Laws for the
Ordering of National Labour' of 20 January 1934. The basic labour law
of the Third Reich, the law of January 1934 effectively strengthened the
position of employers: works councils were to be replaced by so-called
'Councils of Trust' to be elected annually from the workforce, under the
'supervision' of the NSBO, and were to act in a purely advisory capacity
to the 'plant leader' i.e. the employer. The law, which was drafted by
Dr. Werner Mansfeld, a civil servant in the ministry of labour who had
formerly been employed by an association representing the interests of
mine-owners, enable employers to draw up their own plant regulations.
Workers were no longer to settle their grievances through negotiation
and, if necessary, industrial action, but rather such grievances were
not to be settled before 'Courts of Social Honour' through which
employers could in theory be punished. It was up to the labour trustees
to decide whether or not a case should be brought before these courts:
and in practise, the courts acted only against smaller employers. The
representative element embodied in the 'Councils of Trust' was abandoned
in 1935, when elections to the councils were abolished after
'unsatisfactory' results.

The DAF was not provided for in the January 1934 law, and its
development was a product of compromise and ad hoc improvisation, within

the framework of as little interference with the 'rights' of employers as possible. In November 1933, Ley had been forced by Hitler to sign a joint statement with the minister of economics, the minister of labour and Hitler's economic advisor, Keppler, stating that: "..The German Labour Front is the organization for all working people without reference to their social or economic position. The German Labour Front is not the place for deciding the material questions of daily working life, or for harmonising the natural differences between individual workpeople".[1]   Early in December 1933, the DAF underwent a thorough-going reorganization along more clearly corporatist lines. Reich Plant Committees replaced the coordinated white- and blue-collar unions which had hitherto formed the organizational basis of the DAF: the new organizations were to contain both employers and workers. Thus, the DAF was not to assume the representative role of the unions it had replaced. As a consequence of his dual position as head of the DAF and Reich organization leader of the NSDAP, Ley was able to strengthen the position of the DAF which gradually expanded into a massive organization with over 26 million members and about 30,000 functionaries. Local DAF officials seem to have seen their activities as an extension of the claim of the party to have reordered social life and transcended class barriers, and in order to give the Volksgemeinschaft some credibility in the eyes of workers, were prepared to bring pressure to bear on uncooperative employers (though, once again, such pressure appears to have been largely confined to smaller firms).

Ley appeared to have achieved one of his aims in October 1934 when it was planned to amend the January 1934 law to increase the power of the DAF at the expense of both the employers and the labour trustees: many DAF officials saw the law as unduly favourable to the employers and the ministry of labour and hoped to weaken the position of both by subordinating the labour trustees to the DAF. Yet the decree signed by Hitler in October 1934, which was to have effected this, was never implemented: neither Hess' office nor the ministries of economics and labour had been consulted, and the need to placate the economics minister, Schacht, and industry, sealed the fate of this proposal. The extent to which industry was able to retain its independence from the DAF after 1933 became clear in March 1935, when Schacht was able to force Ley to come to an agreement with the minister of labour and the ministry of economics, whereby although in theory the employers were abosorbed into the DAF, the office which represented them – the Reich Economic Chamber – was made the economic office of the DAF, and subordinated to the ministry of economics. Thus, the DAF was to be deprived of any role in creating economic policy. Ley attempted in 1936 to reassert the authority claimed for the DAF in the decree of October 1934:   but this attempt failed, as did an even more far-reaching claim in February 1938, which merely succeeded in uniting all the other leading figures in both party and state against the DAF, thereby checking its expansion.

The integrative role of the DAF had been clear from the outset.   Although their organizations had been destroyed, industrial workers still had to be won over to support of the regime. To this end, Ley established two organizations in November 1933 under the aegis of the DAF – 'Beauty of Labour' (Schönheit der Arbeit) and 'Strength through Joy' (Kraft durch Freude). The 'Beauty of Labour' organization sought to persuade employers to improve working conditions in their factories, and launched a series of propaganda campaigns e.g. 'Clean people in a clean plant'. The 'Strength through Joy' organization sought to organize the leisure time of industrial workers - to give the Volksgemeinschaft some concrete social content. Through the organization leisure facilities were made available to a limited number of workers which had hitherto been the preserve of the middle and upper classes e.g. sea cruises. Much was also made of the stated aim of the regime to enable each worker to buy his own family car - the Volkswagen (lit. 'People's car') - Hitler himself laid the foundation stone of the Volkswagen factory in May 1938. 'Strength through Joy' also placed great emphasis on physical fitness - from 1936, physical training and sports facilities were introduced into factories. The DAF also sought to appeal to the pride of the skilled worker in his work through the National Trades Competition (at first intended only for apprentices, but later extended to include all workers) which offered limited possibilities for promotion to the able, and was intended to promote the training of skilled workers, who were essential to the rearmament programme. Thus, the regime attempted to substitute status for material improvements: in the Volksgemeinschaft, class differences had been transcended and the motive for work was the desire to serve the national community rather than any desire for material gain - or so the ideology of the DAF suggested. The ambivalence of the regime's attitude towards labour was reflected in another institution, the labour service Reichsarbeitsdienst, RAD). The origins of the RAD were to be found in the work-creation schemes set up in the final phases of the Weimar Republic as an attempt to relieve unemployment. The Nazi regime soon realised the advantages of such a scheme: in a period of high unemployment, it freed jobs for family men and, after unemployment had been overcome, it provided a pool of cheap labour for agriculture, and also offered the opportunity for pre-military training and political indoctrination, while a young worker was outside of his working-class community. The RAD became compulsory for all (male) youths in 1935, and since all youths, regardless of class, were affected, the regime could make propaganda capital out of the implied egalitarianism of the scheme.

How did workers respond to the destruction of their organization? How far did they accept the alternative organizations established by a regime which had achieved power on the basis of promising to destroy organized labour?

IV. The Change from unemployment to full employment through the impact of the rearmament programme:

For many workers, employment must have seemed the most vital question. The SPD and the socialist unions had seemed unable to protect their jobs, and by 1933 those workers without jobs saw employment as their chief priority, those with work sought guarantees that they would remain employed. The labour trustees cooperated with employers during the early years of the regime to keep wages at or below their 1933 level: the presence of a large pool of unemployed workers, who acted as a labour reserve, assisted this. The period 1933-6 is characterised by increasing state intervention in the labour market - but intervention which almost always benefitted employers over and against workers, by relaxing work regulations and increasingly attempting to regulate the labour market. Thus, in July 1934 a decree was enacted enabling employers to amend regulations on maximum working hours, and a series of

decrees increased the extent to which the regime intervened directly to
allocate labour. The ministry of labour assumed control of the labour
exchanges, which were granted a monopoly in the supply of labour in
August 1934. The regimentation of labour went a step further in
February 1935, when workers were issued with 'work books' containing a
record of their qualifications and previous employment, which were also
noted by the labour exchanges, thus facilitating the direction of labour
resources. This period was also characterised by the solution of the
unemployment problem - the level of unemployment fell from just over 6
million (registered) unemployed in January 1933, to just over 1 million
in August 1936 on the eve of the introduction of the Four Year Plan.

The development of the labour situation from mid-1936 onwards
must be seen in the light of the massive rearmament boom which the
regime initiated. Between 1933 and 1939, Reich expenditure rose about
fourfold and the Reich debt about threefold. The vast bulk of this
increase is to be accounted for in terms of the expenditure necessary to
finance the rearmament programme. The GNP of Germany more than doubled
during this period - from 58 mrd. RM in 1932 to 130 mrd. RM in 1939:
yet even as a proportion of this increased GNP, expenditure on armaments
rose from 1% to 23%. In the wake of the rearmament boom and the Four
Year Plan, there arose an acute labour shortage. If 1936 is taken as
the base level (= 100), the level of employment in Germany rose from
60.5 in 1932 to 125.1 on 1939. The increased level of employment was
most striking in those industries related to rearmament. Thus, in the
iron and steel industry, the index rose from 27.2 in 1932 to 149.3 in
1939: in the engineering industry, from 44.3 in 1932 to 145.1 in 1939:
and in the electrical industry, from 55.1 in 1932 to 145.3 in 1939.
Total employment rose from 13.4 million in 1933 to 17.6 million in 1936,
and had reached 20.8 million by 1939. Unemployment had fallen below the
0.5 million level by late 1938, and the last peace-time estimates for
unemployment in July 1939 put the number of jobless at a mere 74,000.
Yet as early as May 1938, there had been scarcely any untapped sources
of labour amongst the registered unemployed: rather those who were
registered as jobless were either in the process of changing jobs and so
were unemployed for only a short time, or were employable only to a
limited extent (the physically and mentally handicapped, for example).
In late 1938, the Reich labour ministry estimated that there were a
million vancant jobs.

Although the labour shortage had become general by late 1938,
a critical state of affairs had existed in the building and
metal-working industries for at least nine months before this. In the
most obvious ways, by 1939 the labour shortage was hampering the attempt
to expand the armament-related industries further. For example, in
summer 1939, a group of central German munitions factories were crippled
by a shortage of 3,000 workers: these vacancies could only be
two-thirds filled - and this only after a long delay. Similarly, a
factory to produce rubber and synthetic fuel for the Wehrmacht, whose
construction had been ordered by Karl Krauch, the plenipotentiary for
Chemical Production under the Four Year Plan, and which should therefore
have been given priority, was still short of 13,000 building workers in
August 1939. The Four Year Plan Office, under Goering, attempted to
intervene directly in the labour market as early as November 1936, and a
decree of February 1937 made the hiring of skilled and semi-skilled
metal-workers dependent on the prior approval of the labour exchanges.

Yet by June 1938, Goering felt compelled to introduce a decree which empowered the authorities to conscript workers for tasks which were considered to be essential – employers might be asked to surrender a proportion of their workforce. This measure eventually involved the conscription of 900,000 workers – most of whom were employed in the construction of the West Wall.

V. The problems created by the labour shortage

Yet the problems associated with the labour shortage had more far-reaching effects on the economy. One consequence of the labour shortage was a considerable rise in real wages after 1936. Thus, between December 1935 and June 1939, the average hourly rate for industrial workers rose by 10.9%: because of the increased amount of overtime being worked, the rise in average weekly earnings was 17.4% over the same period. Industry was so confident of the continuation of government contracts and the profits which could be gained thereby, that the 'poaching' of workers by rival firms became commonplace. Workers were enticed from one job to another by the offer of a wage increase or concealed fringe benefits – concealed because of the (unsuccessful) attempt by the regime to contain wage increases. Almost any fit worker was now guaranteed a job. The consequences in terms of work-discipline and productivity rapidly became apparent. Falling work-discipline and declining productivity characterised German industry by 1938-9. In the two industries where productivity could be most easily measured –in mining and the building industry – productivity fell sharply in 1938-9. Sickness leave rose as did absenteeism. Absenteeism had become a problem as early as Christmas 1936. In December 1937, Goering created five more paid holidays per year – yet many workers still overstayed their Christmas leave. The gravity of the wage situation is clearly shown by a decree on wage rates issued by Goering in June 1938: the labour trustees were empowered to set maximum wages in particular branches of industry designated by the ministry of labour, and employers breaking these guidelines could be sentenced by the courts to unlimited fines, or even to periods of imprisonment.

The wider consequences of the coincidence of a rise in real wages and the security of full employment, threatened the whole economic strategy of the regime. The idea of a planned economy in which the material situation of all social groups was subordinated to the over-riding aim of rearmament, demanded the cut-back of the consumer sector. To a certain extent, this was achieved by the regime – for example, foreign exchange credits were allocated to the production goods sector of the economy rather than to the consumer goods sector. The rise in employment in the consumer goods sector of the economy was not as spectacular as in the armaments-related sectors. Thus, (1936 =100) the index of employment in the consumer goods industries rose from 78.5 in 1932 to 115.7 in 1939. As a proportion of the net national product, personal consumption in Germany (63%) ranked above only Japan and the USSR, and well below Britain (79%) and the USA (84.6%). Yet even granted this, the size of the consumer goods sector was still too large to be compatible with an economy completely subordinated to the aim of rearmament. Investment in the consumer goods industries reached its highest level of the inter-way years in 1937-9: and on the eve of war, the purchasing power of consumers was higher than it had been in 1929. Granted the inadequate supply of consumer goods, this had the effect of setting up further inflationary pressures within the economy.

VI The domestic 'crisis' of 1938-1939:

It has been argued that as a consequence of the internal development of the German economy between 1936 and 1939, the regime was confronted in 1938-9 with a massive economic, social and political crisis. As a consequence of the rearmament boom there had arisen fierce competition between firms in the production goods sector of the economy, and between this sector and the consumer goods sector, for increasingly scarce raw materials supplies, foreign exchange credits and skilled workers. This crisis was compounded by the increasing problems of meeting obligations on the massive Reich debt, and a crisis in agricultural production, stemming largely from the flight of poorly-paid agricultural workers into better-paid jobs in industry. The whole complex of problems which arose as a result of the labour shortage threatened the continuation of rearmament at the existing level, let alone further expansion of the armaments-related industries. At root, it has been argued, the crisis stemmed from the inherent contradiction between the foreign policy objectives of the regime (and the rearmament necessary to achieve these objectives), and the weak support for the regime among industrial workers. The regime was unable to create a 'rational' hierarchy of economic priorities which would involve the subordination of all human and material resources to the aim of rearmament, since this would have entailed a massive reduction in the production of consumer goods, and the enforcement of a draconian wage policy. The Nazi regime had failed to integrate the industrial working class into the Volksgemeinschaft: although workers could articulate their discontent to only a limited extent through strike action, they were able to exploit their relative scarcity, and the regime felt unable to call for the necessary sacrifices from them. This crisis formed an impasse which seriously restricted the regime's room for diplomatic manoeuvre, and made an alternative strategy of a war of plunder for human and material resources (Raubkrieg) increasingly attractive as a solution to both diplomatic and domestic (economic and political) problems. It is against this background that Hitler's diplomatic initiatives of 1938-9 should be seen, in particular his decision to go to war with Poland in autumn 1939, well in advance of his 'timetable' outlined at the 'Hossbach' meeting of November 1937.

VII. Interpretations of the nature of the crisis:

The evidence for this thesis is not disputed: what is at stake is the interpretive framework which is built around this evidence, and which, to some extent, helps to constitute it as evidence. The author of the thesis, Tim Mason, has been criticised by both German and English scholars for failing to make the analytical terms he is using clear enough. Thus, they argue that the use of the all-embracing term 'working class' (Arbeiterklasse) is misleading: industrial workers, workers in small artisan workshops and even agricultural workers are all portrayed as resisting the policies of the regime to some extent, and since Tim Mason employs a dichotomous social model, groups with different and sometimes even conflicting interests are categorised together. This is clearly a valid criticism: there are enormous difficulties involved in speaking of the 'industrial working class' as a whole - glossing over the differences between workers in different

branches of industry, between skilled, semi-skilled and unskilled
workers, for example - and to broaden the term 'working class' beyond
this is, arguably, to distort it beyond use. Critics of Tim Mason's
thesis further argue that the failure to analyse thoroughly what is
meant by the term 'working class' is paralleled by his failure to
analyse clearly what is meant by the term 'system of rule'
(Herrschaftssystem) in its broadest sense. To argue that the crisis of
1939 stemmed from the 'fusion of the capitalist economic system and the
political dictatorship'[2], surely demands an analysis of the balance of
these two elements? The nature of the state in capitalist society is
not clear, even within the Marxist tradition of analysis within which
Tim Mason stands. It might be argued that the dichotomous social model
used by Tim Mason is an ideal type in the Weberian sense, and that it is
concerned with economic and social power, rather than with social
stratification. Further, that the crisis of 1938-9 was an inevitable
consequence of the regime's rearmament policies granted the internal
logic of a capitalist economy. However, even these answers to
criticisms of the thesis are not without their problems, and, in any
case, they need to be brought out more clearly if the thesis is to gain
widespread acceptance.

Similarly, if the definition of class proposed by E.P.
Thompson and adopted by Tim Mason - '.. class happens when some men as a
result of common experience (inherited or shared) feel and articulate
the identity of their interests as between themselves, and as against
other men whose interests are different from (and usually opposed to)
theirs' - is to be accepted, it becomes necessary to examine not only
what workers were confronted by (political dictatorship, the capitalist
economic system) but also how they perceived their situation. Class is
a statement about both the objective economic and social position of a
group within a society and its economic system, and about how this
position is experienced and perceived by that group (if this were not
the case, the whole distinction between class in-itself and class
for-itself, would have to be abandoned). This point is especially
significant, since most western political sociologists would stress the
limited nature of the capacity of workers in a capitalist society to
build up a systematic analysis of systematic exploitation. Moreover,
industrial sociologists are inclined to see phenomena such as
absenteeism and low productivity as essentially individual reponses to
the work situation, lacking the wider social awareness which would make
them political activities. It is an open question as to how far
industrial workers were able to maintain a sense of class identity in
the absence of representative working class institutions, and to act in
accordance with this feeling. Even if it were established that
industrial workers felt a class identity and that absenteeism, etc.,
should be seen in this light (and this is extremely unlikely in the
light of the source material available) it would not follow that only
one construction could be placed on this. Workers in the USSR were
similarly oppressed during the period of capital accumulation for Soviet
industrialisation in the 1930s - we are ill-informed as to their
repsonse, but the regime certainly felt obliged to introduce exemplary
coercion to discipline the workforce. The action of workers in Eastern
Europe more recently (especially in Poland) bears all the hall-marks of
class action: what are such workers struggling against - working and
living conditions? the absence of democratic representation of their
interests? the political hegemony of the communist Party? Clearly not

the capitalist economic system!!

It is in the light of these problems that the position of the working class within the economy and German society during the Second World War assumes its importance. The extent to which the regime was able to subordinate all material and human resources to the war economy, and the extent to which the labour force was mobilised for the war effort act as indicators of the extent to which the regime was able to win the support of industrial workers. Tim Mason has argued that the immediate pre-war years were characterised by an increasing level of coercion, which affected all classes and groups within society, but especially the industrial working class. Thus, the Gestapo appears to have become involved in maintaining labour discipline i.e. productive relations: 'labour education camps' were established and workers who were found guilty of, for example, unjustified absenteeism, might be sentenced to short, sharp spells of punishment. The development of the relations between the working class and the regime and industry, is thus of central significance not only for the development of German society during the war period, but also will influence the way in which we regard the opposition of industrial workers to the sacrifices called for by the regime in the pre-war period.

VIII. Labour policy during the war:

With the outbreak of war in September 1939, the regime introduced a series of measures under the general cover of the 'war economy' decree of early September 1939. All holiday benefits for workers were abolished and the 'poaching' of workers became more difficult since the offering of fringe benefits (concealed wage increases) was made illegal. Higher rates of pay for Sundays, nights, and overtime working were abolished. Morever, the labour trustees were empowered to fix maximum wage rates and working conditions in all branches of industry: the fixing of wage rates was difficult to implement, and so in October 1939 they were simply frozen. On top of these measures, the regime introduced a war-time income tax which affected about 40% of all industrial workers. If fully implemented, these proposals would have led to a fall of about 10% in real industrial wages. It was planned that this decrease should be mirrored by a fall in prices throughout the economy, except in agriculture. Yet these measures were vigorously opposed by the industrial workforce. The whole of German industry was affected by the tactics of passive resistance adopted by industrial workers. The poor work-discipline which had characterised German industry on the eve of war now reached chronic proportions – one official described the situation in terms of 'sabotage'. In the face of this campaign, the regime was forced to back down. In mid-November 1939, the bonus rates for Sunday, night, and holiday-working were restored, and workers were compensated for the holidays they had missed since September. Although these concessions were qualified by an increase in the rate of taxation for industrial workers, the regime had clearly been forced to back down in the face of mass opposition and withdraw unpopular measures. By Decmeber 1939, almost all of the September programme had been withdrawn – overtime rates were reintroduced for work in excess of the six eight-hour shifts per week regarded as standard: and in September 1940, full pre-war overtime rates were reintroduced. Thus, it seems that the pre-war limits to the demands for material sacrifices which the regime could make of the working population continued into the war period.

It was inevitable that the labour shortage which had arisen by 1939 could only become more acute during the war, as conscription into the Wehrmacht reduced the number of men available for work in industry. Most of the belligerent nations overcame the labour shortage problem through two innovations in the work-process. On the one hand the increased employment of women in industry: and on the other, the rationalisation of production techniques, and the introduction of labour dilution - whereby complicated industrial work was broken down into its component tasks which could then be performed by semi-skilled or unskilled workers with special machine tools. In Germany, the first solution was not adopted: and the second was, as far as can be seen, only partially implemented. Rather, the German war economy became increasingly dependent on the employment of foreign workers, of whom there were 7.1 million in Germany by June 1944. Most of the foreign workers eventually employed in Germany were already there by May 1943; thereafter, coercion from the occupied territories became more difficult. By May 1944, foreign civilian workers and prisoners of war made up 29.3% of the total industrial workforce, and 22.1% of the total agricultural workforce. Civilian foreign workers were employed increasingly in the armaments industry - by November 1944, they made up 31% of the total workforce in the airframe industry where the repetitive and assembly-line nature of the work meant that unskilled or semi-skilled workers could easily be employed. Similarly, by this date, more than 25% of the total workforce in the machine-building and chemical industries was made up by foreign workers. From July 1941, the employment of Russian prisoners-of-war was theoretically possible (though the first contingents did not arrive until November 1941) - the desire of the regime to employ foreign workers in order to maintain the standard of living of the German population overcame ideological barriers.

IX. The failure to conscript women:

Only recently has the failure of the German authorities to mobilise women for the war effort been examined in any detail, in the context of a broader study of the position of women in the economy during the Third Reich. The number of women employed in Britain rose by about 50% in the period 1939-43 - by about 2.25 million. In the USA, the number of female workers rose by about 50% between 1941 and 1945 - by about 6.5 million; and the proportion of the total workforce made up by women rose from 29% in 1941 to 37% in 1944. In Germany, on the other hand, there was never such a mobilisation of women for the war effort. Thus, the number of women in insured employment fell by 6.3% between June 1939 and March 1940. The number of women who were registered as 'economically active' fell from 14.62 million in May 1939 to a low point of 14.16 million in May 1941, and it did not rise above the May 1939 figure until 1944 - it stood a 14.89 million in September 1944. The failure to mobilise women for the war effort was not a consequence of the exhaustion of the available reserves of potential females workers. On the basis of the 1939 census, the ministry of labour estimated that there were 12.42 million women who were capable of work (arbeitsfähig) but who were not actually working (erwerbstätig). Of those who were married, 5.42 million were childless.

There is an almost universal consensus amongst historians that the failure of the Nazi regime to mobilise women for the war industries was a consequence of Nazi ideology, which stressed that woman's place was in the home, and which was opposed to the idea of exposing women to the physical and moral dangers of industrial work; the stock of Aryan women had to be preserved. Yet there is considerable evidence at least to qualify this consensus. The hostility of the Nazi regime to the employment of women in industry was only given concrete form in the shape of government measures and policy statements during the years 1933-4 (the campaign against both a husband and wife earning during a period of high unemployment, against Doppelverdienertum); and in the face of the labour shortage of the late 1930s, the employment of women was actually encouraged. Moreover, from the mid-1930s onwards, the regime drew up contingency plans for the conscription of women in the event of war. For example, in July 1938, a law based on the unpublished National Service Law of May 1935, had provided for the conscription of women into industry so that the vacancies created by the conscription of men into the Wehrmacht might be rapidly filled. Almost all of the groups involved in the administration which would be responsible for labour allocation in the event of war believed that there would be conscription in one form or another: what was at stake was how and where such a conscripted female labour force would be directed. Thus, '.. by the beginning of the war, there existed a legal apparatus which - at least in theory - permitted the comprehensive conscription of all women aged between 14 and 60.'[3] This is hardly evidence of an all-pervasive ideological consensus against the conscription of women into the war industries. Considerable sections of the governmental apparatus at the highest levels accepted the inevitability of conscription; Goering seems to have been particularly closely involved in the matter.

At least some of the reasons for the reluctance of the regime to conscript women into the war industries are to be found in the fear of the regime of the strength of the potential opposition to what was conceded to be an unpopular measure. The general unatttractiveness of industrial work for women before 1939 had been compounded by the poor rates of pay (apart from considerable differentials in pay between men and women, only 4,8% of the female industrial workforce was skilled) and the very limited possibilities for promotion. Moreover, in an attempt to maintain the morale of troops in the field, the allowances granted to the wives of serving soldiers were set at a very high level - up to 85% of the husband's former wages (compared with 36% in the USA and 38% in the UK) - thus removing material incentives for women to take war-work in industry. That considerations of domestic political stability were involved is demonstrated by the debate which took place over the question in the spring and early summer of 1940. In a conference in late February 1940, General Thomas, the Wehrmacht economic chief, had stated: '.. the labour shortage has become the crucial issue of the war.'[4] A vigorous debate then ensued which seemed to conclude with a victory for those pressing for conscription measures to force women to work. Yet the support of Goering (as plenipotentiary for the Four Year Plan) was crucial. In May 1940, he ordered preparations for the implentation of a conscritption decree; but in early June 1940 he stated that he could not sign the decree ".. because it would cause too much unrest among the population".[5] In a subsequent reply to a letter from Keitel, Goering stated that he had been reluctant to sign such a decree since the debate began, and that the war situation (the defeat of France) now enabled him to avoid such a measure.

This debate was to act as a pattern for the treatment of the question of female conscription for the war industries during the rest of the war. The question was twice discussed in 1941, but it was not until the winter offensive of the Red Army in 1942-3 that any form of conscription was introduced. In January 1943, a decree was issued stating that all women aged between 17 and 45 were required to register for work. Yet the lack of success with which this decree was implemented may be judged from a comment from the Speer ministry (responsible for armaments and munitions) in December 1943 : '.. We must record a total failure to mobilise German women for work in the war effort'.[6] At the same time, it became increasingly difficult for those women who were employed to secure the approval of the labour offices to leave their jobs; many simply disappeared. Conscripted women had a notoriously low productivity (many employers were reluctant to accept women conscripted under the January 1943 decree, preferring foreign workers who might be paid less and were more easily coerced) and until 1943 there seemed to be an inexhaustible pool of potential workers in the occupied territories. The role of ideology in hampering the conscription of women must thus be qualified - even Sauckel's oft-quoted memorandum of April 1942 setting out the ideological reasons for not conscripting women, was a reversal of the position he had held before his appointment as plenipotentiary for Labour in March 1942, and concludes by stating: 'I cannot enumerate all the reasons which have led me to this conclusion'.[7] Hitler certainly expressed objections to the conscription of middle-class women for factory work - possibly motivated by an exaggerated petty-bourgeois chivalry toward middle-class women. He may also have been taken aback by the wave of protest from middle-class men which accompanied the January 1943 decree - he was certainly sensitive to charges of introducing 'Bolshevism' into Germany. Articulate middle-class opposition may well have reinforced his own prejudices and convinced him that conscription of women was a highly sensitive issue, and his reluctance to alienate middle-class support may have made it impossible to proceed with a rigorous conscription programme which would have mobilised only the (considerable) reserves of working-class women who were not working in the war industries - there was already bitter feeling (accurately reflected in the SD public-opinion reports) against non-working middle-class women amongst those working-class women who were trapped in industrial work by the legislation of 1938-9.

X. The politics of labour allocation - the Armaments Ministry versus the Party:

The development of labour mobilisation policies must be seen within the framework of the overall development of the war economy. Whether through fear of the social and political consequences which might follow, or as a result of deliberate strategic planning, at no time before 1941 was Germany committed in any serious way to the move towards a total war economy, in which all human and material resources would be subordinated to production for the war effort. Rather, the period 1939-41 was characterised by the persistence of single-shift working (thus failing to make the fullest possible use of available capital equipment), and a slight shift away from the consumer to the

production goods sector in the structure of production. Labour
shortages were partly to blame for the fact that total national output
rose only 6% in the period 1939-42, and the total industrial output rose
by the comparatively low figure of 20%. Other factors also hampered the
increase in arms production – shortages of raw materials being the most
significant. However, the ultimate limit to war production – the size
of the workforce available – was not reached until late 1944. Rather,
in the German case, the problem was one of <u>allocation</u> of the available
labour resources to the various sectors of the economy. The consumer
goods sector of the economy remained important for a much longer period
than was the case in the British war economy. Indeed, even the
cut-backs in consumer goods production which had taken place in 1939-41
were seen as unacceptable by the regime. In June 1942, Hitler ordered
Speer to reduce armaments production and to increase the allocation of
resources to the production of consumer goods. It was only after the
further deterioration of the situation on the eastern front that this
intention was abandoned. In certain cases, the production of consumer
goods actually increased between 1943 and 1944; and as late as October
1943, Speer felt compelled to seek the support of the <u>Gauleiter</u> in
reducing the production of consumer goods. Speer's greatest success in
this area was the reduction of textile production; but he faced the
oppostion of the <u>Gauleiter</u> throughout the war over the wider issue of
cut-backs in consumer goods production.

Each <u>Gauleiter</u> was Reich defence commissioner for his own
<u>Gau</u>, an office which gave him considerable powers. Speer could
neturalise this by using the armaments inspectors as his regional
agents, but only at the cost of arousing considerable oppostion. With
the support of Bormann, the <u>Gauleiter</u> were often able to oppose the
attempts of the Speer ministry to 'rationalise' industrial production at
the expense of the consumer goods industries. Hitherto, explanation of
these developments has been in terms of the 'institutional Darwinism'
which is held to have characterised the Third Reich, and the desire of
the individual <u>Gauleiter</u> to maintain their independence possibly with
the aim of making their <u>Gaue</u> independent of fiscal control after the
war. Yet this fails to explain why Hitler supported the arguments of
Bormann and the <u>Gauleiter</u> rather than those of Speer. Possibly there
was more to the struggle, in which one side possessed the advantage of
direct access to Hitler. The oppostion of the <u>Gauleiter</u> to the
reduction of consumer goods production might be found to be based in the
fact that they were more aware than Speer of what was <u>politically</u>
possible, and that it was this argument which enabled them to resist the
demands of the Speer ministry, and enable Bormann, the representative of
the party closest to Hitler, to win the <u>Führer's</u> support for a policy of
only moderate cut-backs in consumer goods production. Hitler had in any
case resisted calls by the military for a shift to a total war economy
before winter 1941; and the reports of the Four Year Plan office on the
economic situation always included the opinion that it was necessary to
procede cautiously – an opinion based on the evidence of the Berlin
President of Police. It was in response to proposals from another
would-be centraliser that <u>Gauleiter</u> Burckel commented in January 1942
that the Third Reich suffered from a superfluity of <u>administrators</u> and a
dearth of <u>politicians</u>.

Despite an attempt to rationalise the way in which exemption
from conscription was applied to skilled workers, the process of labour

allocation remained a confused one. Nominally, labour allocation was
under the control of state secretary Syrup at the Reich labour ministry;
yet effectively it was in the hands of ministerial-director Mansfeld who
simultaneously held the post of commissioner for labour supply in the
Four Year Plan organization. It was to overcome the problems faced by
the labour ministry when trying to move workers from one Gau to another
(mainly the opposition of the Gauleiter), that Speer welcomed the idea
of a plenipotentiary for labour supply. Speer's candidate, Karl Hanke,
Gauleiter of Lower Silesia, was not appointed however; Bormann's support
secured the appointment of Fritz Sauckel, Gauleiter of Thuringia; all
the interested parties wished to see Ley excluded from the post.
Significantly, both of the main candidates for the post were Gauleiter,
and so were presumably aware of the importance of political
considerations when dealing with labour questions. Speer was at first
content with Sauckel's appointment, and Sauckel for his part was an
advocate of thorough-going labour mobilisation - including the
mobilisation of women. It was only after he abandoned his draconian
first programme for labour mobilisation, after long discussions with
both Hitler and Goering, that his relations with Speer began to
deteriorate. Sauckel allocated labour on the basis of different
criteria to those proposed by Speer (economic 'rationality') and
strongly defended the right of the Reich Labour Offices to allocate
labour at the regional level (Speer sought to control the allocation of
labour at the regional level through the regional armaments
authorities). Speer never gained control of labour allocation and, from
late 1943 onwards, faced mounting demands from both Hitler and Goebbels
for wholesale conscription, which invariably resulted in the
conscription of men Speer regarded as vital for the war effort. The
final defeat of Speer's policy came in November 1944 with the
establishment of the Volkssturm (a form of levée en masse) to be raised
by the Gauleiter (who controlled the very few exemptions) but to be led
in action by the Wehrmacht.

XI. Relations between the working class and the regime during the
    war:

        If the German working class has appeared as an oject of the
policies of the Nazi regime during the war, rather than as an actor in
its own right, this is largely because we know so little about the
reactions of German workers to the demands made upon them by the regime.
It has been suggested that the development of the war economy can be
fruitfully analysed if the failure of the regime to win the support of
industrial workers before 1939, and the limitations this placed on the
ability of the regime to mobilise all resources for the war economy, is
presumed to be valid for the way period; and that the capacity of the
Gauleiter and the party generally to win the support of Hitler in his
role as arbiter, lay in his concurrence with their argument that the
plans for economic mobilisation suggested by the Speer ministry would be
politically unacceptable. Yet we have little information on the ways in
which the actual or supposed feelings of workers affected policy-making
decisions at the Reich level, except through the reports of the security
service, the SD (Sicherheitsdienst) and by analogy with the pre-war
period. The crucial question is: to what extent was the industrial
working class won over to support the regime during the war period, and
to what extent was there the same kind of consensus amongst all classes
as to immediate war aims as there was in Britain?

Applying the criteria used for the pre-1939 period, a small increase in productivity is found for the war years, of the order of 10-12%. This is lower than in other belligerent economies, yet it might be partly as a consequence of the reluctance of industrialists to rationalise their capital equipment for the highest production of goods essential to the war effort. The restriction of shift-working might also be a consequence of workers' opposition or of technical problems. Clearly the balance of these two factors must be assessed; but this can only be done after empirical research into all aspects of the war economy, which we lack at present. Following the official wage statistics, it seems that the high-point of the average number of hours per week worked was reached as early as September 1941 (49.5 hours per week) and declined thereafter (to 48.3 hours per week in March 1944). After the war, leading figures in the Speer ministry were to comment on the very restricted use of shift-working. Speer himself was alarmed at the persistence of single-shift working in the crucial area of the machine-tool industry. Thus, a survey of 260 firms - representing over 80% of the industry - showed the 89% of workers were working one shift only. The working week in the machine-tool industry rose from 50 hours per week in 1940 to 57 hours per week in 1944; yet only where urgent orders or repair work had to be completed was a 70 hours week attempted. The use of double-shift working was hampered by shortages of skilled workers (who, as a proportion of the total workforce in the machine-tool industry declined from 51% in 1940 to 27% in 1944) and supervisory staff.[8] Wage statistics appear to be less ambiguous than those surrounding working hours and productivity; between 1939 and 1944, weekly earnings rose by 9.6% - compared with an average increase of 80% in Britain between October 1938 and July 1944, and up to 90% in the metal-working, engineering and ship-building industries. On the other hand, the methods used to finance the war economy (the attempted wage freeze, and the measures to place the assets of the banks, etc., at the disposal of the regime) suggest the reluctance of the regime to tax the working class.

The failure of the potentially explosive inflationary pressures within the German economy to materialise during the war, may be atttributed in part to the effective insulation of the German economy from that of the rest of Europe through various economic mechanisms; but the failure of the industrial working class to make use of the methods of passive resistance it had used before the war (and against the September 1939 programme) to improve its material situation, might be attributed to the extension of the coercion of industrial workers, which had already become clear before 1939.

After the destruction of the KPD and SPD, the attention of the _Gestapo_ turned increasingly to workers who were designated as 'anti-social' and hostile to the regime. Thus, in March-April 1938 and again in June 1938, large numbers of 'work-shy' workers were rounded up for internment in concentration camps. The object of the arrests was firstly the elimination of persons '.. who are a burden to the community and therefore do it harm'; but also to satisfy the need for labour - '.. the strict implementation of the Four Year Plan demands the employment of every able-bodied person and does not permit anti-social individual to avoid work and thereby sabotage the Four Year Plan'.[9] In this context, the designation of the SS as an instrument to maintain the domestic political structure in a personal instruction issued by Hitler in August 1938, is significant. The domestic coercive role of the SS was extended in September 1939, when it was empowered to carry out summary executions of particular categories of persons arrested under the 'Principles of internal protection of the state during wartime' issued by Himmler. That the SS was considered as an agent of domestic coercion is clear from the 'Statement on the future of the Armed State Police' issued by Hitler in August 1940 : '.. the Waffen-SS formations will return home having proved themselves in the field and so will have the authority required to carry out their duties as state police'.[10] In 1941, Himmler ordered the establishment of so-called Arbeitserziehungslager (labour education camps) - though this largely formalised the existing situation; such camps had been in operation well before 1939. The increasing use of the SS as a coercive agent within the Reich is clear from the figures based on the daily reports of the Stapoleitstellen (local police) of all arrests made in October 1941. For the pre-September 1939 Reich alone (i.e. excluding the areas of Poland directcy annexed in 1939, Austria, and the so-called Bohemian-Moravian Protectorate) there were 10,776 arrests, and over 75% of these (7,729) were for 'avoiding work'. Similarly, between January and June 1944, 13,000 German workers were arrested for either 'ceasing work' or 'avoiding work'. A thorough investigation of the coercive role of the SS within Germany during the war remains to be carried out; but in the light of the above evidence, it seems plausible to suggest that the importance of domestic coercion increased significantly during the war years and was a major factor in preventing the emergence of a mass opposition to the regime along the lines of the mass opposition to the Wilhelmine state which emerged in 1917-18. It also seems possible to suggest that the increasingly important role of the SS as an agent of domestic coercion, played a role, hitherto neglected, in explaining the expansion of the 'SS State' during the war. The ability of the regime to continue to maintain relatively high standards of living during the war as a consequence of the wholescale plunder of the occupied territories is also of importance in attempting to explain the apparent absence of popular opposition to the regime during the war. Once again, it will only be possible to assess the balance of the two elements of the regime's policies towards the industrial working class - coercsion and concession - after detailed research on the social history of the war period has been carried out.

XII. Conclusion

The most significant conclusion of any study of the relationship between the industrial working class and the Nazi regime, is that the regime failed in one of its basic aims - that of abolishing class conflict, and integrating German society into a Volksgemeinschaft. The form of this continued conflict - the extent of workers' conscious opposition to the regime, as opposed to simply exploitation of a favourable market situation - is still a matter of dispute. However, what is no longer at stake is that workers were able to exploit their favourable market situation after 1936 to improve their material situation, regardless of the regime's rhetoric of sacrifice in the interest of the Volksgemeinschaft. It is also clear that domestic economic, and therefore political, considerations played a hitherto underestimated role in the foreign policy calculations of the regime, in 1938-9. The response of the regime to a basically indifferent or even hostile work class - a mixture of concession and coercion - reflected its weak political base. This pattern continued into the war period, and domestic political considerations may have lain behind the decision not to conscript women for the war industries, and the corresponding coercion of millions of foreign workers. The failure to shift to a total war economy and Hitler's support for the <u>Gauleiter</u> may also be seen as a response by the regime to its weak political base in the industrial working class. The ambivalent and hesitant nature of the regime's policies towards the industrial working class was also reflected in the increasingly important role of coercion within German society during the war.

This analysis has broader implications for the whole way in which we regard the institutional structure of the Third Reich. That 'institutional anarchy' characterised the Third Reich, is by now a commonplace; but too often this anarchy is portrayed as being simply a consequence of the irruption of an 'irrational ideological party' into the 'rational bureaucratic' procedures of the civil service, state apparatus, etc. A basically Weberian analysis is taken over wholesale, often without even acknowledgement of its origins. The failure of the regime to mobilise women for the war effort, the use of foreign workers whose productivity was low, the reluctance of the <u>Gauleiter</u> and the party in general to support Speer's 'rational' programme for labour allocation, have all been described in these terms. Yet this analysis fails to provide any <u>motor</u> for institutional development within the Third Reich - unless to fall back on the notion of 'Hitler's court' - a misty realm cut off from the dynamics of a capitalist society. It has been suggested in this article that the essential starting point for any examination of Nazi society and economy as a whole, is the acknowledgement of the persistence of what it is convenient to label 'class conflict', albeit in forms which are often hard to track down and evaluate, and that the history of the institutional development of the Third Reich must also be firmly rooted in the acknowledgement of this fact.

Notes

1. See T. W. Mason <u>Sozialpolitik im Dritten Reich</u> (Opladen, 1977), pp.115f.

2. Mason <u>Sozialpolitik</u>, p.313.

3. D. Winkler <u>Frauenarbeit im Dritten Reich</u> (Hamburg, 1977), p.86

4. Mason 'Women in Germany 1925-40' in <u>HWJ</u>, 2, p.19.

5. ibid. p.20

6. ibid, p.22

7. For a translation of this memorandum, see J. Noakes and G. Pridham, <u>Documents on Nazism 1919-45</u>, (London, 1974), pp.647ff

8. I am extremely grateful to Alistair Doherty of St. Antony's College, Oxford, for the long conversations we have had on the German war economy. He is currently preparing a doctoral thesis on the German

machine-tool industry during the war, and was kind enough to show me a draft chapter.

9. Broszat in H. Krausnick et al. <u>Anatomy of the SS State</u>, (London, 1968), p.455

10. Buchheim in Krausnick et al. <u>Anatomy</u>, pp.262ff.

BIBLIOGRAPHICAL NOTES

The Nazi Party and the Third Reich : the Myth and Reality of the One-Party State

The only general study of the Nazi Party is: D. Orlow, A History of the Nazi Party 1933-1945 2 vols. (Pittsburgh/Newton Abbot, 1969, 1973). Both volumes contain a vast amount of interesting information in a rather indigestible form. E. N. Peterson, The Limits of Hitler's Power (Princeton/N.J., 1969) has some interesting local detail from Bavaria. J. Grill, 'The Nazi Party in Baden 1920-1945', Ph.D. Univeristy of Michigan, 1975 covers the whole period from a regional angle and provides a useful corrective to some of Orlow's theses.

More work has been done on the party before 1933 than afterwards. Of the numerous regional studies several are in English: W. S. Allen, The Nazi Seizure of Power: the Experience of a Single German Town 1930-1935 (Chicago, 1965/London, 1966) and G. Pridham, Hitler's Rise to Power: The Nazi Movement in Bavaria 1923-1933 (London, 1973) both deal with the seizure of power as well. R. Heberle, Fron Democracy to Nazism. A Regional Case Study on Political Parties in Germany reprint. (New York, 1971) is a brilliant piece of electoral geography; J. Noakes, The Nazi Party in Lower Saxony 1921-1933 concentrates on the development of the party organization. On the background and mentality of the 'old fighters' see: T. Abel, The Nazi Movement. Why Hitler Came to Power, (New York, 1966) and for a statistical analysis of Abel's data see P. Merkl, Political Violence under the Swastika. 581 Early Nazis, (Princeton/N.J., 1975) and see also P. Merkl, The Making of a Stormtrooper, (Princeton/N.J/, 1980). On the background and mentality of the Gauleiter see R. Rogowski, 'The Gauleiter and the social origins of fascism', Comparative Studies in Society and History, 19, 1977.

J. Nyomarkay, Charisma and Factionalism in the Nazi Party, (Minneapolis, 1967), puts forward an extremely suggestive if not always convincing thesis on the organizational dynamics of the party.

On the party after 1933 H. Gerth, 'The Nazi Party: its Leadership and Composition', American Journal of Sociology, XIV, (1940) though in some respects dated is still worth reading. Aryeh L. Unger, The Totalitarian Party. Party and People in Nazi Germany and Soviet Russia, (Cambridge, 1974) contains some stimulating ideas but takes a rather different line from this article.

Among the most important books on the Nazi Party in German are W. Schafer, NSDAP. Entwicklung und Struktur der Staatspartei des Dritten Reiches; Peter Diehl-Thiele, Partei und Staat im Dritten Reich. Untersuchungen zum Verhältnis von NSDAP und allgemeiner innerer Staatsverwaltung. Münchner Studien zur Politik Bd.9, (München, 1969), and P. Hüttenberger, Die Gauleiter. Studie zum Wandel des Machtgefüges in der NSDAP, Schriftenreihe der Vierteljahrshefte für Zeitgeschichte Nr. 19, (Stuttgart, 1969).

Recreating the Civil Service : Issues and Ideas in the Nazi Regime

The outlines of German administrative history can be found in Herbert Jacob, German Administration since Bismarck. Central Authority versus Local Autonomy, Yale Studies in Political Science No. 5, (London and New Haven, 1963). Two contemporary studies of administration under the Nazi regime remain helpful, in default of any more recent historical work: Fritz Morstein Marx, Government in the Third Reich (New York, 1937), and J. K. Pollock, The Government of Greater Germany (New York, 1938). By far the best historical study of the Nazi state is Martin Broszat, Der Staat Hitlers (Munich, 1969), of which an English translation is forthcoming. Although not likely to appear in translation, mention must be made of Hans Mommsen, Beamtentum im Dritten Reich, Schriftenreihe der Vierteljahrshefte für Zeitgeschichte Nr.13, (Stuttgart, 1966), Peter Hüttenberger, Die Gauleiter. Studie zum Wandel des Machtgefüges in der NSDAP Schriftenreihe der Vierteljahrshefte für Zeitgeschichte Nr. 19, (Stuttgart, 1969), and Peter Diehl-Thiele, Partei und Staat in Dritten Reich. Untersuchungen zum Verhältnis von NSDAP und allgemeiner innerer Staatsverwaltung, Münchener Studien zur Politik Bd.9, (Munich, 1969). Mommsen's essay 'National Socialism: Continuity and Change', in Walter Laqueur (ed.), Fascism. A Reader's Guide, Harmondsworth, (1979), pp. 151-92, is invaluable. Similarly, the monumental tripartite study of the 'seizure of power' by Bracher, Sauer and Schulz remains an indispensable if unwieldy text: Karl Dietrich Bracher, Wolfgang Sauer, Gerhard Schulz, Die nationalsozialistische Machtergreifung. Studien zur Errichtung des totalitären Herrschaftssystems in Deutschland 1933-34, Schriften des Instituts für Politische Wissenschaft Bd. 14, (Köln/Opladen, 1962); Bracher's The German Dictatorship. The Origins, Structure, and Effects of National Socialism Harmondsworth, (1973) summarises some of the approaches and findings of the monograph. The relevant parts of Jeremy Noakes and Geoffrey Pridham (eds.), Documents on Nazism 1919-1945 (London, 1974) are extremely useful, both for its translations of contemporary documents and the editors' commentaries. Edward N. Peterson, The Limits of Hitler's Power (Princeton, 1969) covers some of the same ground as this essay, and also shows in vivid detail what 'administration' meant in practice both to its bearers and its objects. A number of the essays in Peter Stachura ed., The Shaping of the Nazi State (London, 1978) are relevant, as also those in Gerhard Hirschfeld and Lother Kettenacker eds., The 'Führer State': Myth and Reality. Studies on the Structure and Politics of the Third Reich (London, forthcoming). Jane Caplan, 'The Politics of Administration: the Reich Interior Ministry and the German Civil Service 1933-1943', Historical Journal XX, 3 (1977), pp.707-736, contains fuller footnote and source references. Those who are interested in the analysis of the Nazi system from a theoretical angle should look at Nicos Poulantzas, Fascism and Dictatorship. The Third International and the Problem of Fascism, (London, 1974).

Popular Opinion in the Third Reich

The concept of 'popular opinion' in the context of the Third Reich and the strengths and weaknesses of the source material on which any analysis of it must rest are discussed in Marlis G. Steinert, Hitlers Krieg und die Deutschen. Stimmung und Haltung der deutschen Bevölkerung im Zweiten Weltkrieg (Düsseldorf, 1970), and Aryeh H. Unger, The Totalitarian Party (Cambridge, 1974). Selections of the sources have been published in: Martin Broszat et al., eds., Bayern in der NS-Zeit. Soziale Lage und politisches Verhalten der Bevölkerung im Spiegel vertraulicher Berichte (München/Wien, 1977); Robert Thévoz et al. eds., Pommern 1934/35 im Spiegel von Gestapo Lageberichten und Sachakten (Köln/Berlin, 1974); Bernhard Vollmer ed., Volksopposition im Polizeistaat (Stuttgart, 1957); Franz Josef Heyen ed., Nationalsozialismus im Alltag (Boppard am Rhein, 1967); Jörg Schadt ed., Verfolgung und Widerstand unter dem Nationalsozialismus in Baden (Stuttgart, 1976); and for the wartime period Heinz Boberach ed., Meldungen aus dem Reich (Neuwied, 1965). To date there is no edition of the valuable 'Deutschland-Berichte der Sopade', copies of which I used in the Wiener Library, London, and the originals of the regional reports in the Archiv der Sozialen Demokratie, Bonn.

Analysis of opinion has largely concentrated on the war years, for which the central SD reports are available. The most useful study here is that of Marlis Steinert (see above), though the SD reports have also been thoroughly exploited in the unpublished dissertation by Lawrence D. Stokes, The Sicherheitsdienst of the Reichsführer SS and German Public Opinion, Sept. 1939–June 1941 (John Hopkins Univ., 1972), and in Stokes's article based on this thesis, 'Otto Ohlendorf, the Sicherheitsdienst and Public Opinion in Nazi Germany' , in George L. Mosse ed., Police Forces in History (London, 1975).

My own book, Der Hitler-Mythos 1920–1945 (Stuttgart, 1980), attempts to deal with the interaction of propaganda and popular opinion which created and sustained the Führer cult, the integrating function of which I explored in 'The Führer Image and Political Integration: the popular conception of Hitler in Bavaria during the Third Reich', in Gerhard Hirschfeld and Lothar Kettenacker eds., Der "Führerstaat": Mythos und Realität. Studien zur Struktur und Politik des Dritten Reiches (Stuttgart, 1980). Hitler's popularity among the German people is also the subject of Lothar Kettenacker's contribution to the same volume, 'Sozialpsychologische Aspekte der Führer-Herrschaft'.

The economic influences on popular opinion have so far received no exhaustive examination. The valuable documentation and analysis of the position of the working-class in T.W. Mason's Arbeiterklasse und Volksgemeinschaft (Opladen, 1975), casts light on worker attitudes, but little detailed attention has up to now been given to peasant reactions to agrarian policies. Adelheid von Saldern, Mittelstand im "Dritten Reich" (Frankfurt/New York, 1979), fills the gap to some extent for the peasantry and for retailers and craftsmen, and work which I have in preparation contains substantial sections on the Bavarian peasantry.

Studies of the church struggle have not concentrated on its impact on popular opinion, though many touch on it. Sources for a systematic analysis are readily avaiable, many in printed form in, for example, the selections from the reports of the Bavarian Regie´rungspräsidenten in Helmut Witetschek ed., Die Kirchliche Lage in Bayern 1933-1943 4 vols., (Mainz, 1966, 1967, 1971, 1973), and extracts from the central SD reports in Heinz Boberach ed., Berichte des SD und der Gestapo über Kirchen und Kirchenvolk in Deutschland 1934-1944 (Mainz, 1971). Jeremy Noakes provides a valuable analysis of the spectacular Oldenburg affair in 'The Oldenburg Crucifix Stuggle of November 1936: a case-study of opposition in the Third Reich', in Peter Stachura e´d. The Shaping of the Nazi State (London, 1978); the Bavarian 'fight for the crosses' of 1941 has so far received no equally detailed treatment, though there is a relevant short section in Edward N. Peterson, The Limits of Hitler's Power (Princeton, 1969). A summary of the growing opposition to the 'euthanasia action' can be found in Steinert, pp.152ff.

On the 'Jewish Question' there is again a useful short section in Steinert (pp.236ff), which deals with the war years, as does the article by Lawrence D. Stokes, 'The German People and the Destruction of the European Jews' in Central European History, 6 (1973). My own article, 'Antisemitismus und Volksmeinung. Reaktionen auf die Judenverfolgung', in Martin Broszat und Elke Fröhlich eds., Bayern in der NS-Zeit II. Herrschaft und Gesellschaft im Konflikt (München/Wien, 1979) concentrates on Bavaria. The perspective is widened to the whole of Germany in my paper on 'The Persecution of the Jews and German Popular Opinion in the Third Reich', forthcoming in The Leo Baeck Institute Year Book, XXVI (1981).

There is still much work needed, both on the areas sketched out in this paper and on the many aspects of popular opinion which I have had no space here to consider. Some of the most important research will in due course be published in the further planned volumes of Bayern in der NS-Zeit, summarising the results of the major project 'Widerstand und Verfolgung in Bayern', directed by the Bavarian State Archives and the Institut für Zeitgeschichte, Munich.

Class Harmony or Class Conflict ? The Industrial Working Class and the National Socialist Regime 1933-1945

This guide to further reading will concentrate on those books which are available in English and reasonably accessible to under-graduates. However, T.W. Mason, Sozialpolitik im Dritten Reich, (Opladen, 1977) and M. Broszat, Der Staat Hitlers (Munich, 1969) are of absolutely fundamental importance to any consideration of the working class in Nazi Germany.

On the relationship between the NSDAP and the industrial working class before 1933 see: T. Childers, 'The Social Basis of the National Socialist Vote' in Journal of Contemporary History 4, 1976. J.

Noakes, <u>The Nazi Party in Lower Saxony 1921-33</u> (London, 1971) and G. Pridham, <u>Hitler's Rise to Power: the Nazi movement in Bavaria</u> (London, 1973) establish the middle class electoral constituency of the NSDAP.

D. Schoenbaum, <u>Hitler's Social Revolution</u> (London, 1966) is an important text for the social history of the Third Reich, though it does not consider the period after 1939. Some of Tim Mason's analysis is available in 'Labour in the Third Reich 1933-9' in <u>Past and Present</u> 33 (1966).

On the development of the German economy after 1933 see: W. Carr, <u>Arms, Autarky and Aggression: A study in German foreign policy</u> (London, 1972). B. A. Carroll, <u>Design for Total War: Arms and Economics in the Third Reich</u> (The Hague, 1968) is also important. A recent survey of the vast literature on 'fascism' is M. Kitchen, <u>Fascism</u> (London, 1976). but also see: T. W. Mason 'The Primacy of Politics' in: S. J. Woolf ed., <u>The Nature of Fascism</u> (London, 1968).

Good surveys of the sociology of industrial conflict are: F. Parkin, <u>Class Inequality and Political Order</u> Paladin, (1971); M. Mann, <u>Consciousness and Action among the western working class</u> (Macmillan, 1973); R. Hyman, <u>Strikes</u> Fontana, (1972); P. Dubois <u>Sabotage in Industry</u> Penguin (1978); I. Meszaros ed., <u>Aspects of History and Class Consciousness</u> (London, 1971).

On the war economy generally, see: A.S. Milward, <u>The German Economy at War</u> (London, 1965); A.S. Milward, <u>War, Economy and Society 1939-45</u> (London, 1977); A. Speer, <u>Inside the Third Reich</u> (1969). E. Homze, <u>Foreign Labor in Nazi Germany</u> (Princeton, 1967) is the best account of the foreign labour programme implemented by Sauckel. The economic empire of the SS is dealt with in sections of H. Krausnick et al., <u>Anatomy of the SS State</u> (London, 1968), which remains the best account of the SS as a whole available in English.

There exists no detailed study of the relationship between the working class and the Nazi regime during the war, but on the failure to mobilise women for the war industries, T.W. Mason 'Women in Germany 1925-40; Family, Welfare and Work' in <u>History Workshop</u>, 1 and 2 is suggestive. J. Stephenson, <u>Women in Nazi Society,</u> (London, 1975), is also helpful - though not as comprehensive as its title might suggest.

Biographical Notes

Dr. Jeremy Noakes is Reader in Modern European History at the University of Exeter. Author of The Nazi Party in Lower Saxony 1921-1933 (OUP, 1971), co-editor (with G. Pridham) of Documents on Nazism 1919-1933 (London, 1974, and New York, 1975). He has also written several articles on Nazi Germany.

Dr. Jane Caplan is a Fellow of King's College, Cambridge. She is the author of several articles on the civil service in Nazi Germany and her book on this subject will be published by OUP in the near future.

Dr. Ian Kershaw is a Senior Lecturer in History at the University of Manchester. Author of Der Hitler-Mythos 1920-1945 (Stuttgart, 1980). He also has a book on popular opinion in Nazi Germany appearing in English shortly, to be published by OUP.

Stephen Salter graduated from Exeter University in 1978. He then spent a year at St. Anthony's College, Oxford. He is currently a Hanseatic Scholar at the University of Hamburg where he is engaged in the preparation of a doctoral thesis on the mobilization of the workforce in Germany during the Second World War.